RELIGION AND T

Current and forthcoming titles in the Classical World Series

Classical World Series

RELIGION AND THE GREEKS

Robert Garland

Bristol Classical Press

General Editor: John H. Betts
Series Editor: Michael Gunningham

Cover illustration: drawing of symposium
by Anna Waern-Sperber, Uppsala University, Sweden

First published in 1994 by
Bristol Classical Press
an imprint of
Gerald Duckworth & Co. Ltd
The Old Piano Factory
48 Hoxton Square, London N1 6PB

Reprinted, with corrections, 1995

A catalogue record for this book is available
from the British Library

ISBN 1-85399-409-X

Printed in Great Britain by
The Cromwell Press Ltd, Melksham, Wiltshire

Contents

List of Illustrations

All attempts were made to seek the copyright-holders of the illustrations, and in some instances they remain unknown.

Acknowledgements

The author would like to thank Dr John Betts for reading the manuscript and for making invaluable comments.

for Robert Wilson

Preface: How Greek Religion Didn't Work

I can think of no better way to begin than by providing a kind of negative catechism of everything that mainstream Greek religion wasn't, in order to demonstrate how it differed from the religious systems with which we are probably most familiar:[1]

> There was no dogma.
> There was no set of beliefs to which everyone had to subscribe.
> There was no 'official' interpretation of religious observance.
> There was nothing resembling a church with a centralised hierarchy.
> There was no concept of conversion.
> There was no absolute distinction between the sacred and profane.
> There was little notion of sin or redemption.
> There was no rule of life.
> There was no denial of worldly pleasures.
> There was little fear of eternal damnation.
> There was no barrier between religion and ordinary life.

We also lack any sacred literature explicitly describing what the Greeks believed and did, akin to the Koran or the Book of Common Prayer. All we have is a collection of highly unrepresentative works produced by some of the least typical minds of the period, whose perspective on religion can only be described – to put it mildly – as original. These include the poems of Homer and Hesiod, the plays of the tragedians Aeschylus, Sophocles and Euripides, and of the comic dramatist Aristophanes, the speeches of orators like Antiphon, the histories of Herodotus and Xenophon, and the philosophy of Plato. We also have inscriptions from gravestones and public documents, vase-paintings, artefacts found in tombs, votive offerings, and the archaeological remains of sanctuaries.

1. The 'catechism' does not apply to Orphism, Pythagoreanism and the Mystery religions, which we shall examine in chapters 17 and 18.

I have tended to concentrate on Athens in the Classical period because that is where most of the literary evidence is to be found. The Hellenistic period, which succeeded the Classical, is also very rich in documentation for the study of Greek religion, but it is of an epigraphical nature and not so readily available to students. I have also cited frequently from Homer, because his influence, like that of Hesiod, was both universal and persistent. Herodotus acknowledged this by stating, 'It was Homer and Hesiod who composed theologies for the Greeks and gave the gods their titles, defined their honours and skills, and described their appearance' (2.53).

What lay at the heart of Greek religion? At the basic level, an almost infinite variety of cults, numbering probably at least ten thousand as far as Athens alone is concerned. We know that Athena, for instance, was worshipped under about fifty different cult epithets (e.g. Polias, 'Of the *polis* or city', Boulaia, 'Counsellor', Parthenos, 'Virgin', etc.), and that each epithet described a different aspect of her power. A pious polytheist would have spread his favours around. In Euripides' *Hippolytus* Hippolytus' exclusive devotion to Artemis and total rejection of her rival Aphrodite were not an acceptable posture to adopt because there was nothing inconsistent about worshipping *both* a goddess who embodied sexual abstinence *and* one who embodied carnal desire. Despite their bewildering diversity, the vast majority of cults were practical, finite and worldly in orientation. Their aim I would sum up as: 'How To Get Ahead'. They sought to enable individuals and states to become more prosperous, more happy and more successful. It was only the 'alternative religions', such as Pythagoreanism, Orphism and the Eleusinian Mysteries, which placed some emphasis on adherence to a moral code. Even in their case, however, it is difficult to draw a distinction between morality on the one hand, and purity of a formal and ritualistic nature on the other.

The aspect of Greek religion that we can most easily investigate was primarily civic in orientation. The financial outlay on state festivals was indeed considerable, as we know from inscriptions relating to the Dionysia and Panathenaia, which marked the high-point of the Athenian calendar. But Greek religion was by no means exclusively played out in the public arena. Whenever Greeks came together as a group, whether as a household, a group of friends, a kin group, a deme or a tribe, they invariably formed a religious association.

One scholar of religion, William James, has written that to study religion one should study the most religious man at his most religious moment.[2]

2. *The Varieties of Religious Experience* (Gifford Lectures).

However, charismatic religious leaders (like the evangelist Billy Graham) were virtually unknown in the Greek world. As an inclusive religious system, it had little need of evangelism. To the extent that charisma played any part at all in Greek religion its effects were probably confined to marginal figures like the seer or *mantis*.

We should also note that the office and competence of a priest extended no further than the enclosure-wall of his sanctuary. The holding of a priesthood could not therefore advance the career of an aspiring politican. The older, so-called gentilician priesthoods (i.e. priesthoods reserved exclusively for members of a *genos* or noble kin-group) were hereditary appointments, while democratic ones (i.e. priesthoods available to the entire citizen body) were filled by lot. In contrast to Rome, where Julius Caesar used the senior office of *pontifex maximus* as a stepping stone to political office, the senior Athenian religious magistrate, the *archôn basileus* or king archon, was elected by lot from 487 onwards. There was therefore no point whatsoever in becoming a religious official unless the supervising of ritual and other duties of a formal nature provided one with personal satisfaction.

Perhaps the most important difference between 'our' sense of religion and 'theirs' is that virtually every Greek, whether male or female, slave or free, was involved to some degree, since every group of individuals tended to think of itself as a religious association. At all periods of Greek history it was much more common to hold the belief that the gods don't care about human beings than to be an atheist. In Britain, by contrast, according to the latest census taken in 1989, only 3.7 million adults attend the established church on a regular basis. That is less than one tenth of the whole population and it represents a decline of 10% over the last decade. (In the USA the percentage of regular churchgoers is around 30%.)

In conclusion, we should note that the Greeks, who had a word for most things, didn't have a word for 'religion'. So the phenomenon which we shall be talking about is something that the Greeks would have had difficulty in identifying as a distinctive aspect of their lives. To them, almost everything was both sacred and profane. Incidentally, polytheism still continues to hold a fascination over the contemporary mind. An example is Gaia theory (Gaia means 'Earth' in Greek), which claims that the earth is a kind of organic being – an idea which is as old as Hesiod.

The Olympian Family

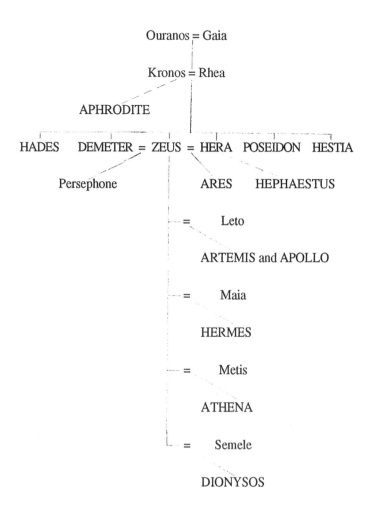

(- - - - indicates descent from a single deity)

Chapter 1
Olympian Suprematism

The Olympian gods are eternal but they have not existed for ever. Zeus, Athena, Dionysos and the rest were all born at a moment in time. That is also true, of course, of Christ, although as a part of the Trinity there is a sense in which He always existed. The Olympians are a dynasty which happens to be in power now and might at any moment be displaced. Zeus, 'the father of gods and men' as he was called, ousted his own father Kronos, who tried to swallow him alive immediately after birth because of a prophecy that his son would overthrow him. Kronos was thwarted by his wife Rhea, who gave him a stone to swallow instead. Evidently the old gods weren't terribly bright! Though each god was born, each is deathless and ageless. Their lives are caught in a time warp, so to speak. So Zeus is destined always to be middle-aged and Apollo to be always on the brink of adulthood.

Fig. 1 Dionysos.

Divine limitations

The Olympians inhabit a universe which was created by primordial beings such as Chaos (Gaping Void), Gaia (Earth), Nux (Night), Ouranos (Sky) and Okeanos (Ocean), who are mentioned in Hesiod's *Theogony*. Being anthropomorphic, which means 'having a human shape', they are inevitably subject to the same needs as we are. Though they are larger, stronger, and more beautiful than us, they are neither omnipotent nor omniscient, and still subject to convention or natural law. When Zeus is minded to snatch Sarpedon, his favourite, from the jaws of death during the Trojan War, his wife Hera cautions him as follows:

> Most terrible son of Kronos, what have you said? Do you wish to save from wretched death a man who is mortal, who was fated long ago to meet his death? Go ahead. But not all the gods will approve. I'll tell you something else and you think about it. If you wish to send Sarpedon to his home still alive, bear in mind that some other god will want to send his own son away from the fierce conflict. For there are many sons of the gods who are fighting around the great city of Priam, and you will arouse great resentment among them.
>
> (Homer, *Iliad* 16.440-9)

Hera's point is that although Zeus can violate natural law if he chooses, he will have to answer for the consequences. This will take the form of a revolt on the part of all the other Olympians.

In addition to the Olympians and the chthonic or underworld deities, whom we shall consider in the next chapter, there was also a multitude of unidentified and unidentifiable divine spirits or half-deities known as *daimones* (singular *daimôn*), who were increasingly held responsible for bad fortune, perhaps in part out of a desire to avoid offending a particular deity.

The gods and justice

At the very beginning of the *Iliad* Apollo inflicts a plague upon the Greek army in order to signal his displeasure with Agamemnon, its commander-in-chief, for having abducted the daughter of his priest. Though Agamemnon is thus guilty of a criminal offence, as far as Apollo is concerned, his fault lies in the fact that the king has personally insulted him. It is not justice, therefore, that spurs the god into action, but hurt pride.

Again, consider the argument between Agamemnon and Achilles that occurs later in the first book. Achilles feels insulted by Agamemnon because he has been deprived of his 'prize', a girl called Briseïs. So he demands 'honour from Zeus'. That is the phrase which is used time and time again. Not, we should note, justice from Zeus, but honour from Zeus. And does Zeus give it to him? He does, but not because there has been some breach in the moral or social order but because Achilles' mother, the sea nymph Thetis, is owed a favour by Zeus.

In Homer's *Odyssey* we sense the emergence of a link between justice and the gods. We are told that Odysseus deserves support from the gods because he sacrifices to them (1.65-7). In other words, Odysseus is worthy of favour because he is pious and god-fearing, rather than because he is a just ruler or a loving father or a devoted husband. Athena, it is true, subsequently praises Odysseus for his justice and kindness as a king (5.7-12), but the real reason why she cherishes Odysseus is because he's a crafty liar and a swindler – just like herself (13.290-9). At the very end of the poem, after Odysseus has slaughtered all the suitors and some of his slaves with the help of Athena, a connection between the gods and justice is made, when Odysseus' father Laertes declares, 'Father Zeus, indeed you gods still exist on high Olympus, if truly the suitors have paid for their reckless insolence' (24.351f.).

In Hesiod, however, justice and Zeus are virtually identical. One of the poet's most passionate utterances is the following:

> You kings, take note of justice. For the immortal gods are close to men and take note of all those who oppress others by crooked judgements and pay no attention to the gods. Upon the boun-teous earth there are thirty thousand guardians of mortal men appointed by Zeus, and these guard judgements and wrong deeds as they roam over the earth, draped in air. The daughter of Zeus is the virgin Justice, honoured and revered among the gods who inhabit Olympus, and whenever anyone hurts her by telling a slanderous lie, immediately she sits beside her father, Zeus, son of Kronos, and speaks of man's unjust mind, until the people pay for the recklessness of their princes, who, plotting evilly, pervert justice by giving crooked verdicts.
>
> (*Works and Days* 248-62)

But Hesiod's view of Zeus is decidedly eclectic, which brings us back to the fact that there are no 'typical' texts for the study of Greek religion.

This testimony apart, it seems that the Olympians were mainly concerned with human justice and morality only insofar as these impinged upon their dignity as divine beings. The chief crimes with which they were concerned were impiety and perjury. And the point about both these crimes is that they diminished the majesty of the gods. In other words, the gods took them personally. It is obvious that impiety diminished their majesty, but why perjury? The answer is that the gods were invoked as witnesses when taking a solemn oath. To break an oath was therefore to take the names of the gods who had been invoked in vain. Crimes such as theft, murder, embezzlement, assault, rape and so forth, hardly concerned them at all.

The gods and morality

The primary reason why the gods could not be the upholders of the moral order is that they simply were not qualified. Their track record was lousy. Zeus' behaviour as a husband was abominable. He seduced at least one hundred and twenty women who are known to us by name. When 'sweet desire' takes hold of him in *Iliad* 14 and he wants to go to bed with his wife Hera, he proceeds to list numerous women with whom he has had casual affairs. None of them, he claims, aroused him as much as Hera does then – hardly the most diplomatic compliment to pay to one's wife (14.313-28)! On one occasion when he became angry with his wife he put handcuffs on her and suspended her between earth and sky with an anvil attached to her feet (*Iliad* 15.18-21).

The gods were all-too-human. That is to say, they were petty, mean-spirited, spiteful, vindictive, deceitful, greedy, and licentious. They were everything (i.e. in the eyes of the Greeks) that the average human being would be – if he was given the chance. Euripides particularly chose myths for his dramas which showed the gods in a reprehensible light. There can be little doubt that his intention was to highlight how morally repugnant the gods were. As K.J. Dover (*Greek Popular Morality*) has expressed it, 'However much we humans may regret that compared with deities we are feeble, ignorant, ugly and smelly, we have no reason to feel guilty about being human; on the contrary, each of us can nourish a secret pride in the ability, by and large, to be nicer than deities.'

Paradoxically, the immorality of the gods ensured that the ordinary Greek felt an intimacy with the divine that is virtually unparalleled in any other religion. The scene in *Odyssey* Book 8 in which the faithless

Aphrodite is caught in bed with her lover Ares by her husband Hephaestus might appear blasphemous in our eyes, but it was certainly not
intended to be by the poet nor interpreted as such by his audience
(266-366). Homer's treatment is the forerunner to the ludicrous portraits
of the gods that we encounter in satyr-drama and comedy. These culmi-
nate in the figure of Dionysos of Aristophanes' *Frogs*, who is so afraid
when he visits Hades that he messes his pants. We need to make a
distinction between comic mockery, which was a sign of affection, and
the rationalising blasphemy which one meets in Euripides, where the
argument seems to be, 'If the gods behave like this, they cannot be gods.'

The gods and pity

To what extent did the gods really care about human beings? It is obvious
that they cared about their favourites, as Athena does for Odysseus, or
Zeus for Sarpedon. But do they care about the great undifferentiated
mass of humankind? Not much, if at all. Although they occasionally
expressed pity for the sufferings of mankind, these are just conventional
platitudes. The attitude of Homer's gods is neatly summed up in these
words uttered by Apollo to Hephaestus, when the latter is urging him to
fight:

> Earthshaker, you would think I was out of my mind if I were to
> fight with you for the sake of wretched mortals, who are like
> leaves, now flourishing and growing warm with life, and feed-
> ing on the fruit of the earth, but then fading away and dying. So
> let us give up this quarrel at once and let mortals fight their own
> battles.
>
> (*Iliad* 21.462-7)

The sentiment that the gods are indifferent to human welfare is a
persistent strand in Greek religion, occurring in Aristophanes' comic
play *Wealth*, which raises the serious question why wicked people
prosper and good people suffer hardship.

    The apparent indifference of the gods to human suffering could
also be given a sinister interpretation. In Herodotus, Solon, who was
celebrated for his wisdom, tells Croesus, king of Lydia, that the gods are
envious of human happiness (1.32). Therefore one should call no man
happy until he is dead because one could not predict what evil the gods
might have in store for him. 'In many cases', Solon concludes, 'the god
gives man happiness and then utterly destroys him.' That's a pretty

depressing view of the gods. Great good fortune was very likely to invite reprisals from a jealous deity because it often produced excessive pride. The lyre-player Thamyris, for instance, was blinded because he tried to rival the Muses, and Marsyas, the inventor of the double flute, was flayed alive by Apollo for challenging the latter to a musical contest which Marsyas lost.

The world as perceived through the eyes of Greek religion was not a comfortable one. The gods were generally indifferent to the human predicament at the best of times, hostile and vindictive at the worst. This was true even in the case of their favourites. When Helen protests to Aphrodite that she has no wish to go to bed with her abductor Paris, the goddess issues this stern warning: 'Don't provoke me, wretched woman, lest I become angry and abandon you, and hate you as much as I now love you beyond measure' (*Iliad* 3.414f.). In order to understand the qualitative difference between a relationship with a Greek deity and the Christian God, we may note the hurried exit which Artemis makes in Euripides' *Hippolytus* when her favourite is dying. She justifies her callous behaviour on the grounds that it is not permitted by divine law (*themis*) for a deity 'to look at the dead or to sully her eyes with the expirations of the dying' (1437f.). In conclusion, the Greeks did not worship their gods because they upheld justice or were supremely good beings. They worshipped them because they were powerful and because it could be extremely dangerous not to worship them.

Chapter 2
Gods of the Underground

Chthonic religion is in essence the antithesis to Olympianism in that it involves the worship of supernatural beings associated with the earth. *Chthonioi* comprise gods of the underworld, the dead and heroes, but we shall reserve discussion of the dead and heroes to chapter 15. The omnipresent motif of chthonic religion is the snake, since snakes were believed to be generated spontaneously inside the earth. A number of myths indicate that the Greeks believed that chthonic worship was antecedent to the worship of the Olympian gods, and that the latter had sought unsuccessfully to supplant their chthonic counterparts. Apollo Pythios, for instance, is said to have established himself at Delphi by killing a snake called the Python (see p. 42).

Although associated, perhaps foremost, with dark forces, danger and black magic, *chthonioi* were also charged with the ability to guarantee food-production, fertility and regeneration. This is exemplified in the fact that Demeter, goddess of the harvest, is the mother of Persephone, the bride of Hades. The Eleusinian Mysteries, whose central myth was the abduction of Persephone by Pluto and which promised a kind of blessedness to the dead, were thus a branch of chthonic religion, as was the cult of Asklepios, whose divine healing was assisted by snakes (see p. 93).

Chthonic versus Olympian

Apart from the fact that both chthonic and Olympian deities were worshipped in sanctuaries and received sacrifices, in other ways they were radically opposed to one another. Whereas the Olympians were worshipped in a spirit of rejoicing, *chthonioi* were invoked in a mood of fear and despondency. Temples were generally not built to chthonic deities, although round buildings known as *tholoi*, which are found in some sanctuaries such as that of Asklepios at Epidaurus (p. 93; see Fig. 19), may have been consecrated to their worship. The financial outlay made on their behalf was therefore considerably less than that made on behalf of the Olympians.

Though the distinction is not absolute, the latter, with the notable exception of the lame metal-working god Hephaestus, were physically perfect, whereas their chthonic counterparts tended to be loathsome. Hades and Persephone, the rulers of the dead, Hermes Psychopompos (Conductor of souls), who escorts the dead to Hades, and Zeus Chthonios, an underworld counterpart to Zeus Olympios, were recognisably anthropomorphic. Hecate, too, a goddess of sorcery who manifests herself only at night, was generally depicted as a virgin but occasionally as a bird of ill omen (Fig. 2). Whereas the Olympians constituted a family, albeit a somewhat unruly one, the chthonic gods were a motley ragbag of disconnected odds and ends who had no ties of kinship with one another.

Fig. 2   Drawing of Hecate on a lead curse tablet, first century AD.

Finally, the chthonic gods are much less prominent in our sources than the Olympians. There is some suspicion that Homer may actually have suppressed mention of them because he was hostile to their worship. They are hardly more prominent in later Greek literature, however. In the tragedies of Sophocles and Euripides, for instance, we never encounter a single chthonic deity. Although a number of sanctuaries incorporated a chthonic offering place and/or shrine, such as the grave of a hero, like that of Pelops at Olympia, the archaeological evidence for this form of worship is extremely meagre.

Despite the structural and symbolic opposition between these two forms of worship, there were also important areas of overlap. The myth of the abduction of Persephone as told in the 'Homeric' *Hymn to Demeter* suggests a kind of marriage (literally as well as metaphorically) between Olympian and chthonic religion, inasmuch as Demeter contracts to guarantee the harvest on condition that her daughter divide her time for all eternity between Hades and Mount Olympus. It is possible that this myth, like that of the Furies to be discussed next, indicates a genuine attempt to work out a compromise between the two, seemingly incompatible, spiritual realms.

The Furies in Aeschylus' Eumenides

One of the most informative testimonies to chthonic religion is Aeschylus' *Eumenides*, the third play of his trilogy the *Oresteia* which was first performed in 458 BC. The *Eumenides* presents a conflict between Olympian religion as exemplified by Apollo, and chthonic religion as personified by the Furies. It is the duty of the latter, a singularly repellent bunch of old hags, to exact vengeance upon those who have murdered their kin. In other words, they uphold basic family values. In Aeschylus' play the Furies pursue Orestes after he has killed his mother Clytemnestra in revenge for the killing of his father Agamemnon. They have been summoned by the ghost of Clytemnestra, who herself has no power to avenge her own murder (94-116; see ch. 15). They hound Orestes down wherever he goes, following the trail of blood which he leaves behind. From a Christian perspective, it is tempting to regard the Furies as the divine, or rather the demonic, embodiment of a guilty conscience. We should, however, be extremely wary of making facile analogies of this sort because there is no evidence that they symbolised guilt as such at all.

Aeschylus describes the Furies as monstrous obscenities; later illustrative evidence frequently portrays them as black, snake-haired creatures with rasping breath; in Aeschylus their eyes discharge an oozing pus (52-4). We are actually told that their costume was so frightening it caused pregnant women to miscarry. Apollo orders them out of his sanctuary with the following baleful words:

Go to where heads are chopped off and eyes gouged out, to justice and slaughterings, to destruction of seed and the pride of young men, to mutilations and stonings, and to the lamentation uttered by people being impaled.

(*Eumenides* 186-90)

But Apollo, the quintessential Olympian deity, is prejudiced. If the Furies happen to be ugly and offensive, we may argue that this is because the murder of one's own kin is a particularly ugly and offensive crime.

'Eumenides' actually means 'Friendly Ones', which, of course, is a euphemism because the Furies are anything but friendly. The Greeks believed that by invoking these fearsome hags by a benign name they might be able to lessen their evil. At the end of the *Eumenides* the Furies *do* become friendly and agree to make peace with the Olympians, in return for being incorporated into the religious life of the Athenian state. In the closing pageant of the play Aeschylus thus seems to be suggesting not only that chthonic and Olympian worship *can* co-exist peacefully side by side, but also that they are even complementary parts of civic worship.

Chapter 3
Accessing the Supernatural

Christians, Jews or Moslems tend to think of God as a being who is watching over them constantly, whether they happen to be addressing Him or not. The Olympian gods, by contrast, if we could interview them, would probably tell us that they had much better things to do than sit around all day waiting to respond to our prayers. In terms of involvement in human affairs, they remind me of people who have the television on all the time but hardly ever watch it. Though they occasionally become interested in what is going on down on earth, the effort of concentration is really beyond them. The petitioner therefore has to find some way to distract them. As is the case in the *Iliad*, the involvement of the gods in the life-and-death drama of human existence tends to be chaotic, unpredictable and erratic. A further problem is the bureaucratic structure of Mount Olympus. At the beginning of the *Odyssey* the hero of the poem has been languishing on Calypso's isle for seven years before an opportunity is found to secure his release. This only comes about because Poseidon, whose Cyclopean son Odysseus has blinded, happens to be absent from Mount Olympus and so is unable on this occasion to exercise his power of veto.

The task of 'accessing' the supernatural, therefore, fell squarely upon the shoulders of the worshipper, who had to gain the ear of the appropriate deity by intoning a prayer, uttering a curse, providing a votive offering, making a sacrifice or libation, or some combination thereof.

Prayers and curses

A prayer commenced with an invocation to the deity. Because of the multiplicity of divinities that existed, invoking the right one could be tricky. It was therefore necessary to cite the deity's full cultic title and mention his or her favoured haunts. The petitioner then jogged the deity's memory by alluding to favours which the latter had performed in the past. He also cited services which he himself had performed or would perform on the deity's behalf. In this way the relationship between god and human was re-established on a friendly, albeit strictly reciprocal basis. The gods did not do something for nothing and, like us, preferred taking to giving. Last of all came the request itself. The conventional attitude in which to address an Olympian was standing, looking upwards, with both arms outstretched. To address a chthonic god, one would lie prostrate on the ground. A typical prayer is that which Chryses, the priest of Apollo, utters to his god at the beginning of Homer's *Iliad*, when he requests that the latter punish the Greeks for abducting his daughter:

> Hear me, lord of the silver bow, who protects Chryse and sacred Killa and rules powerfully over Tenedos, o Sminthian one. If ever I have built you a pleasing temple or if ever I burnt fat thigh pieces of bulls or goats, bring this prayer to fulfilment. Make the Greeks pay for my tears with your arrows.
>
> (1.37-42)

The power of the gods could also be invoked by a curse. The most famous historical curse was passed by the Athenians against the members of the Alkmaionid *genos* (noble kin-group) for having massacred the supporters of a revolutionary called Cylon in c. 610 BC, when the latter were clinging in supplication to the statue of Athena on the Acropolis. The curse was still in force nearly two hundred years later, as we know from the fact that in 431 BC the Spartans issued an ultimatum to the Athenians to the effect that they should 'expel the accursed one', meaning the Alkmaionid statesman Pericles, if they wished to avert the Peloponnesian War.

Sacrifice

The most effective offering was a blood sacrifice (*thysia*), since the gods were thought to derive pleasure and sustenance from the smoke of the sacrificial victim that rose up to Olympus. There is no better way of entering into the reality of Greek religion than by trying to visualise what a sacrifice was like. Each deity had a favourite animal. Athena liked cows, Demeter liked pigs. In the case of the major state deities we are talking in terms of huge numbers of cattle. At the Great Dionysia in 333 BC, for instance, 240 bulls were sacrificed to Dionysos. That constitutes an enormous quantity of blood, dung and bellowing.

The victims were led up to the altar wreathed and adorned with woollen ribbons and their horns gilded. They had previously been checked for blemishes because if any was imperfect the deity would be offended. The priest recited a prayer and sprinkled the victim's head with

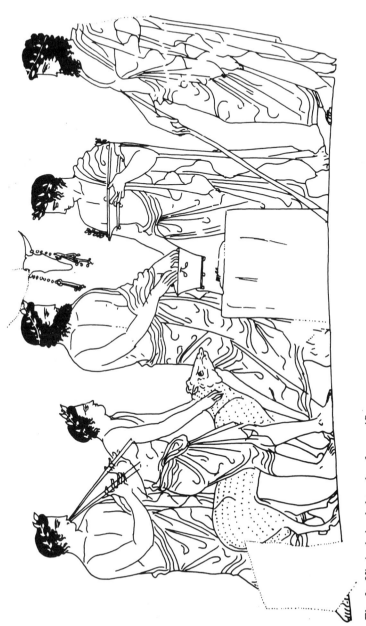

Fig. 3   Victim being led to altar for sacrifice.

holy water. This made the animal toss its head in the air, which was taken as a sign that it went willingly to sacrifice. Barley grains were then thrown on to the altar and the animal's forelock was cut off in an act of consecration. Then, to the accompaniment of a ritual scream (*ololygê*) uttered by the women who were present, the victim was stunned with a blow of the axe and its throat slit. This caused its blood to spurt up in the air and gush over the altar. The entrails were removed and the animal was skinned and roasted, though only a small portion was burnt on the altar in honour of the god. The rest – all, in fact, except for a slice from the thighs rolled in a little fat – was distributed among the priests and celebrants.

Since the thigh-pieces constitute the least edible part of the animal, the chief beneficiaries of a sacrifice were the human participants. Indeed one almost receives the impression that the meal was the most important part of the sacrifice, though we should not think there was anything irreligious in that or that a sacrifice was merely an excuse for a feast. The shared meal was in fact a means whereby men and gods achieved intimacy. Even so, this anomaly troubled the Greeks, so they invented a myth in which they claimed that Prometheus, the friend of man, had set out the parts of the slaughtered animal before Zeus and asked him to choose. Zeus chose the least edible parts, apparently out of compassion for man (Hesiod, *Theogony* 535-57). What lies beneath this comforting story is a fundamental dilemma. Greece is a poor country which cannot support many livestock. Meat was therefore not part of the average person's daily diet and many Greeks would only have tasted it at the great public sacrifices. Hence, the decision to give the gods the thigh bones covered in fat was at root a pragmatic one. In Aristophanes' *Knights* the gods complain that men eat all the best parts of the sacrifice, but they can't come up with a good reason why they shouldn't!

When sacrifices were performed on behalf of the dead or a chthonic deity, the procedure was essentially an inversion of that adopted on behalf of the Olympians. Only female or castrated animals were sacrificed and the preferred colour was black. The victims were slaughtered either over a low altar or directly on the ground so that their blood seeped into the earth. They were burnt whole as a 'holocaust' and dedicated exclusively to the gods or the dead. No portion of the meat was consumed by the living. Finally, sacrifices to chthonic deities and the dead were made at sunset, whereas those to the Olympians were generally performed at dawn. Even in the Classical period the war dead and heroes received blood sacrifices. The Athenians, for instance, annually sacrificed a black bull to those who had died fighting the Persians at the battle of Plataia in 479 BC.

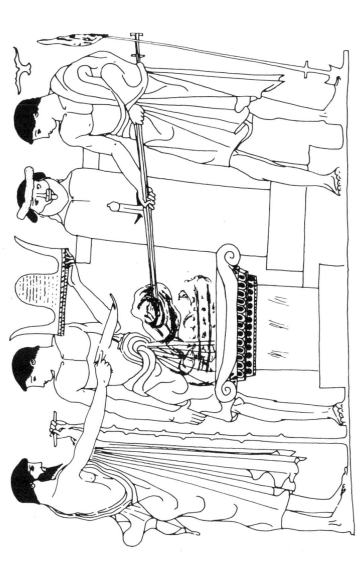

Fig. 4   Roasting of meat on an altar at a sacrifice. The bearded man on the left performs a libation. Note herm to right of centre.

There is plenty of evidence from mythology to suggest that in their distant past the Greeks knew of human sacrifice. In the *Iliad*, for instance, Achilles slaughters twelve Trojan youths in honour of his dead friend Patroklos (23.175f.). But this isn't exactly a sacrifice performed *for* the deceased and Homer doesn't suggest that it is intended to benefit the dead in any way. Rather Achilles slaughters the Trojans as a way of assuaging his grief. Even so, Homer's description seems to preserve the memory of a time when human sacrifice was performed in the Greek world, as has recently been confirmed by archaeological evidence from Crete. Other human victims known to us from myth include Polyxena, who was sacrificed to appease Achilles, and Iphigeneia, who was sacrificed to appease Artemis (see p. 47).

Votive offerings

Votive offerings are gifts which were made either in anticipation or in consequence of divine favour, whether by an individual or by the state. A votive offering could be as small as a figurine or as big as a temple. At the lower end of the scale a humble fisherman would offer a portion of his catch to the gods. At the top end it was customary for a state to make a lavish offering after a victory, which usually consisted of a tithe (known as a *dekatê*) from the spoils of battle. The Sacred Way at Delphi was lined with miniature temples known as 'treasuries' erected by victorious Greek states, the majority of which were paid for by the spoils taken from defeated Greek states. Like sacrifices, votive offerings were a way of ensuring, or more accurately, seeking to ensure that what had happened in the past would happen again in the future.

Fig. 5 Trophy in the form of bronze shield inscribed 'The Athenians from the Spartans of Pylos', dedicated in Athens.

Libations

Libations were poured to the gods or to the dead. Like sacrifices, they were conducted in a very solemn manner. Achilles possessed a special cup reserved exclusively for libations in honour of Zeus (Homer, *Iliad* 16.225-7). The chief ingredients were wine, honey, olive oil, milk and water. There were two kinds of libations, known as *spondê* and *choê*. A *spondê* in the words of Bruit and Schmitt (*Religion in the Ancient Greek City* 39) had the effect of 'placing familiar actions under the protection of the gods'. It might be offered, for instance, when a soldier was leaving home for war in hopes of a safe return (see Fig. 6). At every drinking party or symposium it was customary to pour a *spondê* to the gods in order to ensure that the behaviour of the drinkers did not get out of hand.

A *choê* was offered either to the dead or to the chthonic deities and it frequently excluded wine. The most detailed description of a *choê* is to be found in Aeschylus' *Choephoroi* or Libations Bearers, whose great central episode is an attempt by Elektra to invoke the ghost of her murdered father by pouring pure water onto his tomb (124-51).

Fig. 6 A hoplite warrior preparing to depart. On the right a woman performs a libation.

Failed requests

I have been speaking of sacrifices, votive offerings and prayers as if there were an automatic guarantee that they would find favour. This was not the case. In war, both sides might pray to the same gods but only one can be victorious. An appeal to the gods only met with favour if it did not conflict with the divine will. In the *Iliad* Trojan women place a robe on the knees of Athena and promise to sacrifice twelve heifers in the hope that she will take pity on their city, but the goddess studiously averts her gaze and favours the Greeks instead (6.309-11). In the *Odyssey* Poseidon says he is going to petrify a ship belonging to the Phaeacians and bury their city under a mountain because they have provided safe conduct to his enemy Odysseus (13.149-52). When they see that their ship has been turned to stone, the Phaeacians seek to avert further catastrophe by sacrificing twelve bulls to Poseidon so that 'he might take pity on us and not pile up a high mountain over our city' (182f.). And that's where the poem leaves them, praying to Poseidon and standing anxiously around the altar, awaiting an uncertain future. We can be fairly certain that their prayer will not be answered.

Sophocles provides this gruesome picture of what happens when the gods reject a sacrifice:

> The sacrifice did not catch fire. Instead a putrid slime trickled down, smouldering and spluttering among the ashes. The gall bladder exploded and the dripping thigh pieces were laid bare of their covering of fat.
>
> (*Antigone* 1006-11)

Omens

The sacrifice just described was an attempt to expiate an evil omen sent by the gods. Omens were another important way by which mankind was in contact with gods, though in this case it was the gods who sought to communicate with mankind through signs, which it was the task of a professional seer to interpret. Omens might take the form of anything from a sneeze to an earthquake, from a drop of rain to a solar eclipse. It was an omen in the form of a lunar eclipse which, incorrectly interpreted, delayed the withdrawal of the Athenian fleet from Syracuse in 413 BC, thereby causing the destruction of almost the entire army (see p. 48).

Chapter 4
Divine Intervention

The main areas of human activity and experience that were subject to intervention by the gods were war, agriculture, health, the accumulation of wealth, human fertility, childbirth and safe passage at sea. These are also the areas, we may note, where belief in divine intervention tends to be most pronounced in religious systems the world over. Thus the ability to influence the course of battle is attributed to many divinities, including both the Jewish and Christian God, and Allah. Societies which periodically experience famine commonly endeavour to overcome their fear of starvation by means of festivals designed to ensure a bumper harvest. The ability to heal the sick is for Christians central to Christ's mission and a mark of saintliness in his followers. Although the accumulation of wealth is not something which the Christ of the Gospels offers to his followers, there are present-day Christians who maintain that wealth is a mark of divine favour. Fertility is of major concern in societies where women's ability to conceive cannot be taken for granted and where there is little understanding of the mechanics of reproduction. The high incidence of maternal and infant mortality in the Greek world is reflected in the fact that the Greeks believed that a successful delivery depended on the goodwill of the gods. Finally, safe passage at sea was also thought to depend upon the favour of the gods, due to the squalls that blow up out of nowhere in the Aegean.

Intervention in war

There are many reasons why war is likely to have been the foremost area of divine intervention. One is that the gods themselves had much to gain or lose by the outcome of human conflict and so were inherently fractious. Another is that war is the most dangerous activity engaged in by man. A victory is thus a palpable indication that a state or an individual enjoys the favour of the gods. That is why the Greeks commemorated their victories by erecting temples paid for from the spoils of battle and filled with loot captured from the enemy (p. 16).

Homer's world may serve as a useful starting point for the investigation of the mechanisms of divine intervention, since the involvement of the Olympian deities in the Trojan war provides a model for their involvement in all wars, whether internal, foreign or civil. The poet ascribes to the gods everything that tilts the balance in a battle to one side rather than another – everything in other words that we might identify as 'chance'. On one occasion in the *Iliad* the battle between the Greeks and the Trojans is so evenly balanced that Zeus holds up a set of golden scales to determine which side will prevail (8.68-74). But what is chance but a way of accounting for the inexplicable? When in Book 22 of the *Iliad* Hektor hurls his spear at Achilles and completely misses his target, we can either say that this was just a lousy shot and put it down to chance or we can say it was somehow intentional and credit it to the gods.

The belief that the gods intervened in war was still very much alive in later times, as we see from this passage in Xenophon:

> The gods are obviously now our allies. In clear weather they create a storm when it is to our advantage, and when we are few attacking many they grant us to set up trophies. And now the gods have brought us to a place where the enemy cannot throw their spears and javelins over the heads of the front ranks because their spears and javelins must fly uphill, but we, throwing our spears, javelins and rocks downhill, will reach them and wound many.
>
> (*Hellenika* 2.4.14-15)

Homer's heroes as mind-fields

E.R. Dodds, one of the greatest scholars of Greek religion, in his book *The Greeks and the Irrational* identified three kinds of divine intervention in Homer. The first is 'a temporary clouding or bewilderment of the normal consciousness'. There is an example of this at the very beginning of the *Iliad* when Agamemnon, the commander-in-chief of the Greek army, spitefully robs Achilles, his foremost fighter, of his mistress Briseïs. When the two are reconciled, after a fashion, in Book 19, Agamemnon makes a speech at tedious length excusing his behaviour. The heart of his apology is contained in the following lines:

> I was not the cause of this act [he means the theft of Briseïs], but Zeus and Fate and the Erinys [i.e. Fury] who walks in darkness, in that they cast upon my mind raging blindness (*atê*) in the agora on that day when I took Achilles' prize from him.

But what could I do? It is god who accomplishes all things.
Blindness (*Atê*) is the daughter of Zeus, terrible she is, and she
blinds all men. Her feet are delicate because she does not walk
on the ground but moves over men's heads, bringing harm to
human beings, and ensnaring one or other of them.

(86-94)

Though we do not need to assume that Homer is endorsing Agamemnon's face-saving explanation of his poor behaviour, there is no reason to doubt that belief in *atê* was widespread.

The second kind of intervention involves the communication of *menos* or strength to a warrior during a battle, as when Athena puts a triple dose of *menos* into the chest of the Greek warrior Diomedes. The result is that he was filled with what Dodds calls 'a mysterious access of energy' and was able to perform extraordinary acts of bravery. Somewhat similar is the endowing of a human being with almost superhuman good looks.

The third kind of divine intervention, which is more common in the *Odyssey* than in the *Iliad*, is what Dodds calls 'monitions'. Monitions take the form of a brilliant or foolish idea, the recognition of someone long lost, the sudden remembrance of something, or suddenly forgetting something. The explanation is that the gods, some god or a *daimôn* (i.e. divine spirit), have put the realisation or idea into the person's mind.

Do Homer's heroes have freewill?

Does belief in divine intervention indicate that Homer's gods govern human behaviour to such an extent that his heroes lack freewill? Although many modern readers *do* believe so, there are strong indicators to suggest that this interpretation may not be correct.

Let us look at the opening scene of the *Iliad* when Achilles, in a fit of rage, is on the point of drawing his sword and slicing up his commander-in-chief. His hand is already on the hilt of his sword when Athena suddenly swoops down and grabs him by the hair. Achilles turns and recognises her and asks her why she has come. This is her reply:

I have come from heaven in order to stay your anger, if you take
my advice. The white-armed goddess Hera sent me because she
loves and cares for you both in her heart. Come now, cease from
your strife and do not draw your sword. Merely taunt him with
words, as it shall be. Eventually you will receive three times as

many gifts on account of this hybris. Hold back and obey me.

(1.207-14)

'If you take my advice', Athena is warning Achilles, 'you'll think twice before killing Agamemnon'. Homer's belief in divine intervention does not, it seems, preclude the notion that his heroes have to face moral choices. A deity may seek to intervene to alter the course of events but in order to do so successfully he or she needs the active co-operation of a human agent.

Homer in this passage is attempting to explain why Achilles 'changes his mind' or 'thinks twice' about killing Agamemnon. No one actually knows what happens when a person changes his mind. To us, the phrase 'change one's mind' is a metaphor which we don't take literally. We resort to it because the kind of situation that Homer describes – someone on the brink of doing a violent deed who holds back at the last minute – is very hard to understand. But instead of employing a metaphor, Homer suggests to us that Achilles is the target of 'psychic intervention'. If we wanted to give this a psychological explanation, we could say that he is the kind of person who will suddenly flare up into a towering rage which evaporates for no apparent reason a second later.

A temporary twilight of the gods?

There are indications that by the end of the fifth century a number of Athenians were seriously questioning the gods' ability to intervene in human affairs in order to defend their own interests. In Aristophanes' *Birds*, for instance, when Peisthetairos is regaling Poseidon with the advantages to the gods of making peace with the birds, he cites the type of infractions which the birds will be able to punish and which, so the inference goes, the gods are at this moment powerless to check (1606-25). These include swearing false oaths to which they have been called to witness and promising to make an offering to a god but putting it off with the words, 'The gods wait a long time' (*menetoi theoi*). Likewise in Aristophanes' *Clouds* Socrates puts to Strepsiades the question why Zeus fails to strike notorious perjurors with his thunderbolts, whereas he smites his own shrines and sacred oak trees, adding sardonically, 'though the oak never forswore, I would think' (398-402). This repeated insistence upon the powerlessness and vulnerability of some of Athens' gods hints at the existence of a contemporary debate which is unlikely to have confined itself to the intellectual élite, even though belief in divine intervention remained an article of faith for about another thousand years.

Chapter 5
Doing the Right Thing

Doing the right thing had nothing to do with saintliness or sin. A crucial difference between Christianity and Greek religion is that whereas the former treats sin and wickedness as something separate from and antithetical to the interests and desires of the Almighty, the latter regards sin as something contained within and necessary to the essence of the divine. The Greek gods, in other words, are just as likely to be violent, spiteful and vindictive towards human beings as they are to demonstrate affection, compassion and goodwill.

Piety

Eusebeia, which is usually translated 'piety', means literally 'doing the right thing in regard to *sebas*'. *Sebas*, for want of a better equivalent, is usually translated 'reverence'. *Eusebeia* is proper behaviour towards the gods, one's parents, one's native land and the dead. Porphyry, a late writer, provides us with an exemplary model for popular piety in the person of a certain Klearchos of Methydrion, who, despite his poverty and the insignificance of his city, was singled out by the Delphic oracle as the person who worshipped the gods 'best and most devotedly and who made the most pleasing sacrifices'. Klearchos' recipe for the pious life reads as follows:

> Klearchos declared that he performed the sacrifices earnestly at the appropriate times, on the new moon of each month crowning and cleaning Hermes and Hekate and the other statues which his ancestors had left, and that he honoured them with incense, barley-cakes and wheat-cakes. Every year he took part in the public sacrifices, omitting none of the festivals. At these festivals he worshipped the gods not by slaughtering and butchering victims, but by sacrificing whatever he happened to have, preferably some of the available fruits which he received from the earth, and giving first-fruits to the gods. Some he would donate fresh, others as burnt offerings.
>
> (*On Abstinence* 2.16)

We may note that Klearchos' *eusebeia* is defined exclusively in terms of outward observance. He did the right thing on behalf of the right god at the right time. His piety did not consist in refraining from, say, thinking wicked thoughts about his neighbour. Pope John Paul II has ruled that if a married man lusts after a woman who is not his wife he has committed adultery in the eyes of God. That is not something that a Greek would have understood. His gods did not concern themselves with unrevealed intentions or desires. On the contrary, they left their worshippers largely free to act in their own best interests. The rewards for piety came in this life rather than in the next. Probably no Greek ever acted piously in the expectation, to quote Christ, that he was storing up treasures in heaven.

Piety was one thing. *Deisidaimonia* or 'excessive fear of *daimones*', which is often loosely translated as 'superstition', was quite another. Theophrastus, a pupil of Aristotle who wrote character sketches of Greeks exhibiting what psychiatrists today would call deviant behaviour, provides us with a memorable picture of pathological fastidiousness in relation to religious observance:

> Superstition is cowardice in regard to the *daimonion* and the superstitious man is like this. [When he sees a bad omen] he washes his hands and sprinkles holy water upon himself from a shrine, and walks around all day with a bay leaf in his mouth. If a cat runs across his path, he won't proceed until someone else passes by [i.e. who will therefore be the recipient of the bad omen] or until he has thrown three stones across the road. If he sees a snake in the house..., he calls upon Sabazios [a Thraco-Phrygian god]. If it is a sacred snake he consecrates a hero-shrine on the spot.... He is constantly purifying his home, claiming that it has come under the influence of Hekate. If an owl hoots while he is out strolling, he gets upset and says, 'Mighty Athena' before continuing. He refuses to step on a grave or to approach a corpse or a woman in labour, declaring that it is better that he doesn't become polluted.... When he has a dream he goes to the dream-interpreters, to the seers and to the experts in bird omens, in order to find out which god or goddess he should pray to. Every month he goes to the initiators of Orphic Mysteries in order to be initiated, taking with him his wife or if his wife is too busy, his nurse, and children.... If he sees a madman or epileptic he spits and shudders into his breast.
>
> (*Characters* 16)

Impiety

The word for 'impiety', *asebeia*, makes its first appearance in the sixth century BC in the work of the elegiac poet Theognis who wrote, 'Respect and fear the gods, because this prevents a man from doing or saying anything that is impious (*asebes*)' (1179f.). Impiety covered offences against established religious procedures. It did not include heresy, for which there was no Greek equivalent. That is because the Greek religious system was too disorderly to permit a synthesis of belief along dogmatic lines. In Athens charges of impiety were brought before the senior religious official, known as the *archôn basileus* or king archon (p. xi). Specific charges which were filed under this heading include introducing a new god, parodying the Eleusinian Mysteries, and mutilating statues known as herms (see below).

The most famous impiety trial involved Socrates, who was charged in 399 BC just after the democracy had been restored following its brief suspension under an illegal regime called the Thirty Tyrants. The religious charge against him read as follows: 'Socrates does not recognise the gods whom the state recognises and is introducing new daimonic powers'. In the *Apology* of Plato Socrates claims that he actually does worship the state gods. But he admits as well that he hears the voice of a *daimonion* (little *daimôn*) who tells him not to do certain things (rather than telling him what he should be doing). His *daimonion* was a personal, monitoring voice not wholly unlike a Christian conscience (e.g. *Apology* 40a). Socrates was found guilty and condemned to death. A rather different version of his defence is supplied by Xenophon and it is a matter of debate as to which is the more reliable.

The charge of introducing new gods reflects the fact that the state placed itself under the protection of a particular set of deities. Their number and identity changed over time, but only by decision of the assembly. The fact that many new gods were introduced into Athens at the end of the fifth century does not alter the fact that Athenian religion was inherently conservative (p. 103). Thus Isokrates, writing in the fourth century BC, speaks approvingly of the men of old who:

> …did not irregularly or erratically worship the gods or celebrate their rites. They did not on a whim send 300 oxen to be sacrificed while omitting the ancestral sacrifices. Nor did they celebrate supplementary festivals which incorporated a banquet in an extravagant manner, while doing sacrifices on the

cheap [literally 'from contracts'] when it came to the most sacred of their holy rites. Their principal concern was not to omit any of the ancestral practices and not to add anything that was not traditional. For they recognised that piety consists not in paying out large sums of money but in preserving unchanged the rites which their ancestors had handed down to them. In corresponding manner the assistance which they received from the gods came not irregularly in fits and starts but at the right moment for the working of the land and the harvesting of the fruits.

(*Areopagitikos* 29-30)

That is just one man's view, and a reactionary man's view at that. But the fact that he said it in public indicates that he expected some of his audience to believe him.

Acts of sacrilege were also impious. These could include theft from a sanctuary or the destruction of something sacred, both of which were equivalent to robbing the god. It was a capital offence to cut down the sacred olive trees, for instance, because they belonged to Athena. The most celebrated instance of sacrilege was the mutilation of the herms in 415 BC. Herms were stone pillars which were surmounted by a head of Hermes, the god of travellers (see Fig. 4). They were otherwise in block-form except for a phallus. Herms stood in the streets of Athens and in front of houses to protect private property. Their mutilation, like the parodying of the Eleusinian Mysteries, was committed on the eve of the departure of the naval expedition to Sicily in 415 BC and it understandably caused something of a panic. It is suspected, however, that the panic was fuelled for political purposes, notably to prevent the sailing of the expedition to Sicily.

Betrayal of one's native land was an act of impiety because the gods were implicated in the good of the state. The Greek *polis* or city-state was not just a collection of houses. It was also the home of the gods. So if you did anything to violate their temples and shrines you were committing an act of impiety.

Hybris, excessive pride in one's capacity and good fortune, was also an offence against the gods, although it doesn't quite fall within the sphere of impiety. It may seem curious that the majesty of the gods could be threatened by a mere mortal but it is clear that they did not take kindly to anyone who presented himself as their rival, as we have seen from what happened to Thamyris and Marsyas (p. 6). Hence, the choruses in Greek tragedy are constantly extolling the virtues of keeping one's head down. Even so, if you were phenomenally successful there wasn't much you could do about it. Good fortune could be a curse just as much as a blessing.

Finally, there is one area of behaviour which does not seem to have been regarded as impious, viz. saying insulting things about the gods or presenting them on stage or in poetry in an insulting light. Indeed it is one of the most remarkable features of Greek religion that the gods could be legitimately presented as fornicators, cowards, gluttons and thieves (see p. 4).

Chapter 6
Domestic and Neighbourhood Religion

Up till now I have tended to imply that Greek religion was the concern either of the *polis* or the individual; in other words, that it was either completely public or completely private. That was far from being the case. Any corporate group of individuals, however small, constituted a religious assembly. By corporate group I mean the *oikos* (household or home), the *genos* (noble kin-group), the phratry (brotherhood), the deme (village) and the tribe. Temporary as well as permanent groups also constituted a religious assembly. Thus a symposium or drinking-party, which normally took place in the *andrôn* (men's quarters) of the *oikos*, also functioned as a religious assembly (see Fig. 7).

Fig. 7 Symposium or drinking-party.

The oikos

There is no exact translation of *oikos* into English: it consists of both people and property, including cattle and household slaves. It is the nearest Greek word to 'family', though it only approximates to our word. Its members worshipped together, placed themselves under the protection of the same deities, and regarded their fortunes as linked and interdependent. The head of the *oikos* was its oldest free/citizen male resident, who acted as priest in charge of all the religious practices conducted in the home. Unfortunately our evidence for domestic worship is very meagre, for the simple reason that knowledge of it is taken for granted in our sources. An obvious consequence stemming from the belief that all members of the *oikos* were linked together as a religious community was that their corporate piety was deemed critical to its welfare. Domestic religion thus had the consequence of binding its members more closely together, both slave and free. As such it may have served – I say this only very tentatively – to humanise the relationship between master and slave.

a) Household deities
Principal among the household deities are Hestia, the goddess of the hearth, Apollo Patroös, the god of ancestors, Zeus Ktesios, the god of household property, and Zeus Herkeios, the god of property boundaries. The head of the household supervised the worship of these deities on particular days, attended by all members of the household. The vital importance of family religion is demonstrated by the fact that when an Athenian was standing for magisterial office and the Council was examining his qualifications, they first inquired:

> 'Who is your father and what deme does he belong to? Who is your father's father? Who is your mother and what deme does she belong to?' After that they ask him, 'Do you have an Apollo Patroös and Zeus Herkeios, and if so where are their shrines?' Then, 'Do you have any family tombs, and if so where are they?'
> ([Aristotle] *Constitution of Athens* 55.3)

The ability to give a satisfactory answer to these questions was regarded as proof that the candidate conducted himself responsibly and was fit for public office.

b) Rituals of inclusion

The sphere of domestic religion about which we know most involves procedures that were performed whenever a new 'candidate' was seeking admittance to the *oikos*, such as a newborn baby, a newly-acquired slave, or a bride. The *oikos* was an exclusive and intact unit. It wasn't just a fluid association of random people, any more than a *polis* was a fluid association. Therefore each new candidate had to be inserted into the existing structure in a precise and carefully ritualised way.

In Athens, probably on the fifth day after birth, a ceremony called the Amphidromia was held in the *oikos* of the newborn to negotiate the baby's official entry into the home. I suspect that this was also the first occasion when the new arrival left the *gynaikeion* (women's quarters), to which till now it had been confined with its mother. The Amphidromia bears a superficial resemblance to a Christian baptism, except that it took place in the *oikos*, not in a church or temple, no priest was required to be present, and instead of being baptised in water the child was carried – at a run – around the domestic hearth in order to place it under the protection of Hestia. A 'running around' is the literal translation of Amphidromia.

A bride also had to be admitted to a new *oikos* upon the occasion of her wedding. In fact she passed from one *oikos*, that of her father or nearest ascendant male relative, to another, that of her husband. Ritual had therefore to be conducted in both the *oikoi* of which she had membership. First the bride took a prenuptial bath in her paternal *oikos*, which was also where the wedding feast was held. At the feast she sat with other women, veiled and apart from the men. Then at night the groom conducted her, still veiled, to her marital *oikos*. During the journey the groom sat in the centre, the bride on one side, and the *paranymphos* (i.e. best man) on the other. Hymns were sung in honour of Hymenaeus, god of marriage. Upon arrival at her new home, the bride was showered with nuts and dried fruit, symbols of fertility, and presented with a basket of bread. She then removed her veil and entered the wedding chamber with her husband, while an *epithalamion* (wedding hymn) was sung outside the door.

Domestic religion incorporated much else besides. I have already mentioned that symposiasts constituted a religious unit. Ritual marked the beginning and ending of their 'drinking together' and served to punctuate the stages in between courses. Libations were performed on behalf of a variety of deities in the hope of ensuring that the drinkers did not become disorderly. Finally, the *oikos* played the leading role in funeral rites, as we shall see in chapter 14.

Genos

Religion performed in the *genos*, a noble kin-group whose members traced their descent from a common ancestor, is a branch of family religion that largely became absorbed into the state. All the most venerable Attic cults were *genos*-cults, being administered by *genê* and served by priests who belonged to a specific *genos*. The cult of Athena Polias (Of the *polis*) as well as that of Poseidon-Erechtheus, the two principal state cults of Athens, were both *genos* cults, their priesthoods being hereditary in the *genos* of the Eteoboutadai.

Phratry

Only Athenians of aristocratic descent belonged to a *genos* but every Athenian belonged to a phratry. The phratry was a brotherhood comprising a number of *oikoi*. In the first year of its life a newborn male child was introduced to its phratry at a festival celebrated by each phratry individually called the Apatouria. The infant was presented by its father, who took an oath on the phratry altar that he was 'in very sooth the father of the boy' and that its mother was an Athenian by birth. It was vital for every Athenian boy to gain admission into a phratry because unless he had been accepted into a phratry he could not claim Athenian citizenship. Later, at about the age of 14, he was re-introduced to his phratry and a similar ceremony took place. We do not know whether girls were also admitted to the phratry by a similar rite of inclusion.

Deme

There were literally thousands of cults which were celebrated by the demesmen of each of Attica's 140-odd demes. The deme of Erkhia, which has furnished us with the only sacred calendar that has survived complete, conducted sacrifices on behalf of no fewer than 43 deities and heroes (*SEG* XXI.541, c. 375-50). Deme religion alone could be a full-time occupation, as we learn from a character in Menander's *Bad-tempered Man* who observes contemptuously:

> My mother is going to make a sacrifice to some god or other. She does this every day, touring around in a circle, sacrificing throughout the whole deme.
>
> (260-3)

One of the most important deme festivals was the Rural Dionysia which was celebrated by each of the Attic demes. We gain a vivid if somewhat eccentric picture of this festival from Aristophanes' *Acharnians*, where the complement of worshippers consists of the hero Dicaeopolis, his daughter and two slaves (241-79). During the procession a giant phallus was borne aloft and a hymn was sung to Phales, the personification of the phallus.

I have only skimmed the surface of what is a very large area of Greek religion. But the most important point to grasp is that every group of citizens, however constituted, saw itself as dependent upon and linked to the gods, sought the assistance of the gods in the day-to-day handling of its affairs, and defended its interests as a group by a rigidly upheld principle of exclusion.

Chapter 7
Outlets for Women

The prominence of women in Greek religion is suggested by the important role attached to goddesses who represent an extensive range of female personae, including Aphrodite (sexual love), Artemis (chastity), Athena (masculine womanhood), Demeter (motherhood), Hera (marriage), Hestia (hearth and home) and Hekate (sorcery). Correspondingly there were many religious outlets for women, both as symbols of sexual purity, as priestesses, as celebrants, and as controllers of rites of passage, notably birth and death.

Parts for parthenoi

Parthenoi (virgins) served in many capacities. Each year in Athens two or possibly four young girls of noble birth known as *arrhêphoroi* were selected to reside on the Acropolis and to weave the *peplos* (woollen woman's dress) that adorned the olive-wood statue of Athena Polias, tend her sacred olive tree, and carry certain unspecified objects in a basket balanced on their heads to the shrine of Aphrodite in the Gardens below the Acropolis. Two other *parthenoi* served as *loutrides* or *plyntrides* (washing girls), it being their duty to give the olive-wood statue a ritual scrubbing in the sea.

We also hear of *parthenoi* serving as priestesses or temple servants in expiation for crimes performed by men. The inhabitants of Locri in mainland Greece were required to send two *parthenoi* of aristocratic birth to the temple of Athena in the Troad in expiation for the rape of Cassandra which had been perpetrated by Ajax son of Oileus during the sack of Troy. Pre-marital rituals involving *parthenoi* are also widely-attested. On the island of Keos *parthenoi* were required to remain all day long in sanctuaries playing and dancing under the scrutiny of their suitors, while by night they went from one house to another, waiting upon each other's parents and brothers 'even to the extent of washing their feet' (Plutarch, *Moralia* 249d-e). This somewhat sexist custom seems to have been intended to dramatise the complementary roles of sex-partner and good housekeeper, which a Kean wife, like all Greek

wives, was evidently required to fulfil. Choirs of *parthenoi* were plenti-
ful throughout the Greek world and prominent in religious celebrations.
We have already noted how in Greek mythology the sacrifice of a virgin
is commonly alluded to as a prelude to hostilities.

Priestesses

As a general rule, male deities were served by priests, female deities by
priestesses. This meant that Athena Polias, the most important deity in
the Athenian state, was served by a woman. Though priests and priestesses had little overt power, being primarily in charge of religious
observances and the proper running of their sanctuary, we can hardly
doubt that their office invested them with a certain venerability. This is
particularly likely in the case of Lysimache, who served as priestess of
Athena Polias for sixty-four years and who may well have provided the
model for the outspoken heroine Lysistrata in Aristophanes' play of that
name. The priestess of Hera in Argos was so important that the Argives
and other Greeks used the number of years that she had held office as a
system of chronology (Thucydides 2.1). Apollo's mouthpiece at Delphi,
known as the Pythia, a highly important and revered individual, was also
a woman (see p. 43).

Participation in cults

A number of cults were exclusive to women, just as a number were
exclusive to men. Particularly prominent was the festival known as the
Thesmophoria (see p. 58), the subject of Aristophanes' comedy called
the *Women at the Thesmophoria*, in which a man manages to infiltrate
the Thesmophoria disguised as a woman. Women served as maenads or
worshippers of Dionysos, their activities causing great suspicion among
men, if we are to believe Euripides' *Bacchae*. They also played a part in
cults which were not exclusive to their sex, such as the Eleusinian
Mysteries (see ch. 17). In *Idyll* 15 the Hellenistic poet Theocritus
provides a memorable description of a festival celebrated in honour of
Adonis at Alexandria in the third century BC as seen through the eyes of
two gossipy women called Gorgo and Praxinoa.
      Participation in these cults provided a rare opportunity for female
citizens to congregate outside the home. It is possible that religious
devotion offered psychological as well as social benefits to women,
however, by providing them with an outlet for the frustrations which they
experienced by living lives of virtual seclusion inside the home.

Certainly the grisly description in the *Bacchae* of the *sparagmos* (dismembering of a live victim) and *ômophagia* (eating of its raw meat), which the maenads (literally 'maddened women') perform in order to achieve mystic union with the god, suggests that the cult of Dionysos unleashed frenzy among its worshippers (728-68). However, it should be noted that it is improbable in the extreme that such rituals were current in Athens or indeed in Thebes where the action takes place when this play was produced towards the end of the fifth century.

Midwives

Birth in the Greek world was not perceived primarily as a physiological event but as a ritual requiring the assistance of birthing deities, whose goodwill was judged to be essential both for the production of a viable infant and for the recovery of its mother. It was the duty of a midwife to ensure that the birthing ritual was performed in the correct manner. By administering drugs and intoning incantations or spells, the midwife was believed capable, with the assistance of the deities whom she invoked, of accelerating or allaying labour pains, easing a difficult delivery, and even causing a miscarriage if that were deemed desirable (Plato, *Theaitetus* 149d). Most prominent among the deities whose services she invoked was Artemis, a virgin goddess, who needed to be appeased retrospectively, so to speak, for the loss of the mother's virginity. Also important was Eileithyia, whose name probably means 'She who comes', the personification of a safe and quick delivery.

To what extent the midwife's competence was based upon a sound medical appreciation of the hazards of childbearing and to what extent she served as a mediator between the mother and the birthing deities is impossible to determine, but in view of the fact that physicians rarely presided at a birth her powers must have been very considerable. So far as we know, the only qualification needed to become a midwife was to be above childbearing years.

Tending the corpse and the grave

As illustrations on vases and funerary legislation indicate, women were the principal actors in all the rituals connected with the disposal and care of the dead, as indeed they are to this day in Mediterranean and Middle Eastern countries. It was women who ritually bathed and dressed the corpse, played the leading role in the singing of the lament, and tended the tomb on a regular basis (see ch. 14).

Funerary legislation suggests that women were so demonstrative that their manifestations of grief sometimes needed to be restrained. A law from the town of Iulis on the island of Keos, which is dated to the second half of the fifth century BC, regulated that 'The women attending the funeral had (or, according to another reading, had *not*) to return from the graveside before the men' and that 'Once the burial was over, only women who were polluted were permitted to re-enter the deceased's house. These included the deceased's mother, wife, sisters, daughters, and a maximum of five others' (*IG* XII.5.593). Like festivals, funerals afforded a rare occasion for women to go about in public and so be seen by men. A speech by the orator Lysias describes in a thoroughly realistic manner how an adulterous wife first met her future lover on the occasion of her mother-in-law's funeral (1.8)!

Chapter 8
Pollution and Purification

The Greeks, like ourselves, had a highly developed fear of pollution or *miasma*. Indeed the capacity to distinguish dirt from cleanliness is a basic human instinct that sets an adult apart from a child. *Miasma* was rather like a virus in that it was deadly, invisible to the naked eye, and detectable only in the harm it caused to human beings and animals. And like a virus, it was transmitted by contact so that, unless contained, it could ultimately pollute the entire community. *Miasma* was released in a variety of ways, all of them connected with bodily functions. In ascending order of magnitude and danger, these include sexual intercourse, giving birth, contact with the dead, and involuntary or voluntary homicide. To disperse the *miasma*, rites of purification were performed by purifying priests known as *kathartai*. These were assisted by religious experts known as *exêgêtai* or 'expounders of the sacred law', whose task it was to give advice about the proper procedure to be adopted. The principal purifiers were salt water, fire, disinfectants such as sulphur, and, most potent of all, blood sacrifice.

Sexual intercourse

The historian Herodotus refers to a people who ritually fumigated their private parts by squatting over an incense burner after intercourse, but they were clearly an anthropological oddity in his eyes (1.198). The Greeks performed no purificatory ritual after making love, which indicates that sexual intercourse in their eyes caused only a weak pollution. Inevitably, however, it was forbidden to engage in sexual activity inside a sanctuary, not so much because this was seen as a mark of disrespect to the gods, but because even a weak pollution violated their purity. It is for this reason, too, that sexual abstinence was occasionally enjoined upon worshippers at a festival. A number of cults required priests and priestesses to remain abstinent for a period of time. Only very rarely do we hear of perpetual celibacy being enjoined upon the holder of a religious office, however, as in the case of the Pythia, through whom Apollo made his oracular pronouncements (p. 43).

Childbirth

Sacral laws habitually required priests to avoid contact with women giving birth. We are told that the house in which a birth was taking place had to be smeared with pitch. Photius, a late writer, says that the reason for this was 'to drive away *daimones*', but a more plausible explanation is that the house had to be sealed in order to prevent the pollution from seeping into the community. This practice would also have had the consequence of alerting the community to the danger within. Pollution did not cease once a woman had delivered her child but continued for forty days thereafter, thereby coinciding, approximately, with the cessation of lochial discharge. It seems that one became contaminated simply by entering the house in which a confinement had taken place, irrespective of whether one actually had physical contact with the mother and child.

Death

Death was much more polluting than birth, and with good reason, we may argue, since a dead body spreads disease unless swiftly disposed of. We cannot know for certain, however, whether this was the reason for the discrepancy. Purificatory rituals included bathing the corpse, placing a bowl of water outside the house so that those visiting it could purify themselves upon leaving, taking a bath after returning from the funeral, and so on. Numerous inscriptions from all over the Greek world ban from temple precincts those who have been in recent contact with the dead. The length of time that one was tainted depended in part upon one's kinship with the deceased. Close relatives, whether or not they had actually been in the presence of the dead, were automatically contaminated, at least in some communities. Priests were forbidden all contact with the dead, including presumably those who were close relatives of the deceased.

Involuntary and voluntary homicide

Since homicide released the most intense pollution, an assailant, whether guilty of manslaughter or murder, had to be purified by the most effective means available, namely the blood of a pig. It is almost as if the avenging spirits of the murdered dead required a surrogate victim, though another purpose behind the ritual may have been to bring the assailant once again into contact with blood. It was in order to avoid causing pollution that the Athenians required those condemned to death to take their own life by drinking a cup of poisonous hemlock.

For an insight into what pollution was apparently capable of doing if unchecked we may turn to the beginning of Sophocles' *Oedipus the King*, where a priest, speaking on behalf of the population of Thebes, supplicates Oedipus for his assistance in halting a plague which had been caused by the presence of an undetected killer in the city:

> You can see yourself that our city is in grave distress, unable to
> lift its head from the depths, caught in a rolling swell of death.
> A blight is upon the fruitful plants of the earth, a blight is upon
> cattle among the pastures, and upon the barren pangs of women.
> A god who carries fire, a deadly pestilence, swoops down upon
> our city and ravages it, emptying the house of Cadmus. Black
> Hades grows rich with groans and lamentations.
>
> (22-30)

Oedipus responds by saying that he has sent a representative to Delphi to find out what action Apollo recommends (see next chapter). Back comes the answer: expel the murderer of Laius, Oedipus' predecessor. Only then will the plague abate.

So that we feel the full force of the scene that Sophocles is painting, let me dwell upon this situation for a moment. A man has been killed. He happens to be a king but that doesn't seem to make any difference. Or at least no one in the play says that it does. The man also happens to have been killed by his son, because Oedipus is the son of Laius, though he does not know it, but no one seems to think *that* is the cause of the plague either. The fact is a man – I stress the indefinite article – has been killed and his killer is on the loose. It is the latter's mere presence which is having this terrifying effect upon the community because, quite simply, he is a walking virus.

What I have just described is, of course, not real life but a play. It partakes by definition of unreality. How reliable is it as evidence for belief about pollution among late fifth-century Athenians? In a community as large as Athens, there must have been a considerable number of undetected killers on the loose. Did the Athenians really believe that their presence exposed them to plague?

Arguably a more reliable source of information is provided by lawcourt speeches of the fifth century, especially those of Antiphon who makes frequent reference to pollution. In a speech written on behalf of a young man called Euxitheus who has been accused of murder, the defendant puts forward the following evidence as proof of his innocence:

> It is necessary that in matters of this sort your verdict should be based on signs provided by the gods.... I imagine you are aware that many individuals whose hands were unclean or who were affected with *miasma* in some other way, who have undertaken a sea voyage, have caused their own deaths along with the deaths of those who behave righteously towards the gods. Other innocent people, though they have escaped death, have faced terrible perils because of their encounter with polluted persons.... In my case, however, the opposite has occurred. I have sailed with innocent people and they have enjoyed untroubled voyages. Every sacrifice I have attended has turned out well. I judge these facts to be conclusive proof that the charges brought against me are unfounded.
>
> (*On the Murder of Herodes* 5.82-3)

Did the accused really judge 'these facts to be conclusive'? And if he did, what percentage of the Athenian population shared his belief or were at least prepared to concede it a certain validity, while privately perhaps harbouring reservations about the religious argument? Whatever the answer, it is worth noting that there is virtually no evidence to suggest that a collective historical misfortune was ever blamed on an individual's offence in the way Antiphon suggests. It is easy enough to come to terms with the formal aspects of Greek polytheism but to catch its actual heart-beat is a challenge of a wholly different order.

Chapter 9
Not Just Fortune-Telling

The title of this chapter alludes to the fact that consulting the oracle in the hope of learning about the future was by no means equivalent to the modern exercise of reading one's horoscope in the newspaper. Though I shall concentrate upon Delphi, the main seat of oracular utterance, there were many other oracles throughout the Greek world.

"Apparently I'm a very gullible person who'll believe any old rubbish"

Fig. 8 *Private Eye* (10 September 1993).

Delphi's origin

Delphi is the navel of the world. The Greeks knew that because Zeus had dispatched two eagles from either end of the cosmos to determine the centre of the earth and they met at Delphi. The name Delphi was derived etymologically by the Greeks from '*delphinos*', meaning a 'dolphin', because when Apollo Pythios established his oracular seat at Delphi he guided a Cretan ship to this part of the coast in the form of a dolphin. Incidentally, Apollo was not the first divinity to be worshipped at Delphi. An early poem known as the 'Homeric' *Hymn to Apollo* tells us how he slew a dragon called the Python, from which he acquired the cult epithet 'Pythios'. For this offence Apollo went into exile for eight years as a polluted murderer. The Pythian Games, which were celebrated at Delphi every four years, commemorated this victory. Apollo was consulted not only about the future but also about pollution, since he was the supreme consultant in matters of purification.

Delphi's history

The earliest archaeological evidence at Delphi belongs to the end of the ninth century BC. The boundary wall of the sanctuary dates to the eighth century and the temple is already mentioned in Homer. Delphi's influence was strongest from the eighth to the fourth centuries BC. The oracle gained greatly in importance after the First Sacred War (c. 590 BC), which enabled it to achieve independence from the neighbouring township of Krisa on the coast. Delphi's reputation was so great in the Archaic period that even non-Greeks consulted it. When the temple was destroyed by an earthquake in 548 BC, its reconstruction was financed by Croesus king of Lydia and Amasis pharaoh of Egypt. The contract was given to the exiled Athenian Alkmaionid *genos*, which gained a considerable reputation by using expensive Parian marble instead of the ordinary stone which had been prescribed (Herodotus 5.62; p. 12). Although the oracle – ill-advisedly, as we would think – recommended submission to Persia during the Persian Wars, its prestige did not noticeably diminish as a result. It was only in the fourth century BC that it began to decline in importance, partly in consequence of another earthquake which wrecked the entire sanctuary. Even so, it was still giving out pronouncements in the fourth century AD.

Delphi, being at the navel of the earth, was in the middle of nowhere. Indeed it was its distance from any major centre of power that accounted in large part for its importance since, until the rise of Philip II of Macedon in the 360s BC, it could not be manipulated by a powerful neighbour. From the beginning of the sixth century BC its affairs were run by the Amphiktyonic League or 'the League of those living round about', a council comprising states from central Greece and the northern Peloponnese which met twice a year and ensured the oracle's independence. No fewer than four wars were fought to secure that independence. Delphi itself comprised only a small community of about

1,000 inhabitants. Even so, it was extremely wealthy, not only because of the dedications, but also because of the support services which it provided in the form of taverns and inns.

Oracular procedure

Should we go to war? How can we avert the plague? Should we found a new colony? What should we do now that a religious law has been violated? How can we purify ourselves? These were the type of questions that Apollo would be consulted about by states. But the god also took questions about personal problems. Should I marry? Should I go on a sea voyage? Should I adopt a son? We gain a vivid yet humorous insight into Delphic procedure from Euripides' *Ion*, where a couple consult Apollo about their childlessness. Learning that the first person he meets upon leaving the temple will be his son, the husband accosts one of the temple servants, who understandably rebuffs him!

Before the sixth century BC divination probably took place only on one day of the year, Apollo's birthday. Even in later times there was probably only one day of the month that the oracle could be consulted, and then only in the summer, making a total of nine days per year. Between December and February Apollo resided in the land of the Hyperboreans to the far north and gave no pronouncements. Those wishing to consult the oracle had to pay a fee and then make a sacrifice in the form of a goat. Other preliminary procedures were also required, such as bathing in a nearby spring. The movements of the victim apparently determined whether Apollo was prepared to give answer to a petitioner's question. Inside the temple, or more precisely in the room at the far end of it known as the *adyton* or 'unapproachable place', sat the Pythia, who was the mouthpiece of Apollo and through whom he revealed his answer. In early times the Pythia was a young girl, but later an old woman was selected for the role.

It is here that our evidence begins to run out and where speculations tend to run wild. Simon Price (*Greek Religion and Society* [eds Easterling and Muir] 129) cites the following 'standard' description from the Blue Guide as proof of the kind of fantasising that goes on:

> The Pythia having purified herself, munching a laurel leaf, took her seat upon the tripod which was placed over the chasm in the *adyton*. Intoxicated by the exhalations from the chasm she uttered incoherent sounds which were interpreted in hexameter verse by a poet in waiting. The interpretation, which was always

obscure and frequently equivocal was handed over to the in-
quirer who not seldom returned more mystified than when he
had come.

As Price points out, very little in this description is likely to be accurate.
The evidence for laurel-chewing is extremely late and archaeologists
now believe that there was no natural chasm for the Pythia to sit over.
We shall probably never know how the Pythia became 'inspired', though
the depictions of the mad prophetess Cassandra in both Aeschylus'
Agamemnon and Euripides' *Trojan Women* provide a possible indication
of her behaviour when possessed. The Greeks, of course, believed that
the Pythia was possessed by Apollo. But if we don't believe in Apollo,
how can we come to terms with the mental state of the Pythia?

Interpreting Delphi

When we think of Delphi, it is perhaps natural to think of astrology and
horoscopes. Those of us who continue to admire the Greeks do so in part
because of their rationality and freedom from 'idle superstition', and we
tend to feel embarrassed that a civilization which based itself so much
upon the primacy of reason (as we like to think, at any rate) should have
invested so much trust in such an apparently stupid mechanism for
determining which course of action to follow. Surely there must be a
better way of making up one's mind about a difficult decision than by
returning home 'more mystified than when one had come'?

   Maybe some Greeks who went to consult the oracle *were* looking
for easy answers. But for most of life's problems, easy answers simply
don't exist. And Delphi was not just a lottery – a place to spin a coin in
a ritualised way. That is why the answer that the visitor came away with
was often complex and ambiguous. It was surely not the case that the
god, or the Pythia, or whoever, supplied riddles as a way of keeping
their options open or hedging their bets, as has sometimes been alleged.
The vestibule of the temple at Delphi was adorned with the maxims of
the Seven Sages. Of these the most celebrated were 'Nothing in Excess'
and 'Know Yourself'. Know your limits, in other words, and know
yourself as a human being. We may recall the response that is given to
Oedipus when he goes to Delphi, 'You will kill your father and marry
your mother.' But that's not much help to the poor fellow because he
doesn't know the identity of his parents. In fact what the oracle seems
to be saying is, 'You haven't any sense of who you are.'
   What I am suggesting is that the interpretation of the oracular

message which human intellect, unaided by the gods, had to provide was an integral part of the oracular experience. Take the famous instance of Croesus of Lydia, who is celebrated foremost for his spectacularly wrong interpretation of an oracular response. Herodotus writes:

> Croesus commanded the Lydians who were going to take his gifts to the shrines to ask the oracles (at Delphi and Amphiaraion in Attica) whether he should conduct a military campaign against the Persians and whether he should supplement his army with an allied force. When they arrived the Lydians dedicated their gifts and consulted the oracle as follows: 'Croesus, king of Lydia and other nations, believing that these are the only oracles for mankind, has presented gifts worthy of your divination, and now asks you if he should march against Persia and supplement his army with an allied force.' This is the question they put and both oracles gave the same answer, foretelling to Croesus that if he attacked the Persians he would destroy a great empire. They also counselled him to find out which of the Greeks were the most powerful and to make an alliance with them.
>
> (1.53.1-3)

Croesus duly went to war and destroyed a great empire, just as the oracle foretold. Unfortunately the empire happened to be his own. What a pity he didn't stop to think before jumping to hasty conclusions.

Coming to Delphi and consulting Apollo was not equivalent to renouncing your moral responsibility and saying in effect 'Let Big Brother decide'. It was a journey to the earth's navel in order to deepen one's knowledge and wisdom, particularly, perhaps primarily, one's self-knowledge, upon which factor chiefly depends the successful outcome of any enterprise.

Chapter 10
Making War

We have already seen in chapter 4 that war was the area where the gods were most active in their involvement in human life. No god had exclusive charge of war, as the bewildering multiplicity of deities who were invoked by states at war indicates. The initial cause of war was Eris, Strife personified, who tossed the golden apple into the wedding of Thetis and Peleus and thus indirectly caused the Trojan War. Ares, who is often loosely described as the god of war, was really the god of slaughter. Pythian Apollo was often consulted before states made war, partly because he had access to the future and partly because the future was shaped to some extent by his goodwill. Zeus Soter (Saviour) was invoked when the odds of winning a battle were stacked heavily in favour of the opposing side. His cult was probably introduced in Athens at the time of the Persian Wars in response to the overwhelming odds that the Athenians faced when confronted with the might of Persia. Zeus was actually the general overseer of war, though his powers were limited. What Homer in the *Iliad* calls 'the plan of Zeus' is in effect a plan masterminded by Zeus to secure the temporary defeat of the Greeks with the intention of giving honour to Achilles because of the insult which he has received at the hands of his commander-in-chief (see p. 21). The fact that the plan is not particularly well-thought out or even coherent accurately reflects the uncertainties and unpredictability of war. Athena Parthenos (Virgin) was Athens' private property, so to speak, a veritable war maiden, clad in military attire. Athena Promachos, whose cult epithet means 'the one who fights in the front ranks', was invoked to stiffen the morale of the troops. Pan was the god of the rout who instilled panic into the enemy and caused them to turn tail and flee in disorder. It was he who assisted the Athenians at the battle of Marathon in 490 BC, when, against all odds, their much smaller army succeeded in striking terror into the ranks of the Persians, thereby securing a memorable victory. Many other gods assisted in determining the outcome of a battle.

Virgin sacrifice

A number of myths allude to the sacrifice of a virgin before going to war. Before the Greek fleet could sail to Troy, as we learn from Aeschylus' *Agamemnon*, the king had to sacrifice his daughter Iphigeneia because Artemis was angered by the killing of a pregnant hare in her sanctuary. The hare incidentally was not killed by Agamemnon's soldiers but by two eagles, an act which the seer Kalchas read as an omen indicating that Troy – the pregnant hare – would be destroyed by Agamemnon and Menelaus.

Such myths can support many interpretations. Firstly, we can argue that the sacrifice of Iphigeneia was demanded as a kind of pre-emptive act of atonement for the taking of human life (though in the *Iphigenia in Tauris* Euripides puts forward the novel theory that the victim was spirited away by Artemis just when she was about to be killed). Secondly, the sacrifice provides an excuse for the slaughter that will follow, as if it is the cause of the war and to be avenged by it. Thirdly, it is a kind of ritual blood-letting which serves as a preliminary to the blood bath that is to follow. Finally, the sacrifice of a virgin marks a rejection of love and fertility in preference to war. As such it expresses a commitment on the part of the soldiery to the ethos of war. The fact that Iphigeneia is the king's daughter and that the priest who performs her sacrifice is her father emphasises that this is the ultimate sacrifice. As we have seen, mythological virgin sacrifice was also performed on behalf of the dead, as in the case of Polyxena (p. 16).

There is no evidence that virgins were sacrificed in historical times, but just before the battle of Leuktra in 371 BC the Theban commander Epaminondas is said to have performed a substitute-virgin sacrifice at the tomb of two Boeotian *parthenoi*, who had been raped and subsequently committed suicide out of shame. Their dead father had appeared to Epaminondas in a dream demanding the sacrifice of a virgin as the price for his support but he was prevailed upon instead to accept that of a young filly which opportunely came forward to the altar at the moment the *parthenos* was due to be slaughtered.

Omens, sacrifices and trophies

Before committing his forces to battle, a Greek general ordered his seer to read the omens (see p. 18). The outcome of one of the most crucial engagements in Greek history depended, adversely as it turned out, upon the taking of omens. When in 413 BC the Athenians were ready to depart from Sicily, having failed in their great enterprise to subdue the island, Nikias refused to allow the fleet to sail after an eclipse of the moon had taken place (Plutarch, *Life of Nicias* 23). As a result of the delay, the Syracusans were able to encircle the Athenian encampment with their own forces and bottle up the Athenian fleet in the Grand Harbour. The result was a total massacre.

Solemn prayers were uttered before going into battle. Thucydides tells us that before the departure of the naval expedition to Sicily in 415 BC, the herald commanded silence by a blast of the trumpet, the customary prayers were recited by the crew of the entire fleet in unison, libations were poured from gold and silver goblets, and a paean or victory hymn was sung to Apollo (6.32). Immediately prior to an engagement, *sphagia* (sacrificial victims) were slaughtered. We are told that the Spartans customarily drove herds of goats on to the battlefield which they then sacrificed.

After the battle the victorious side erected a *tropaion* (trophy) on the battlefield at the spot where the most decisive action had been fought. A *tropaion* consisted of an oak trunk decorated with the spoils of victory, consisting mainly of weapons and armour. It resembled, if you will pardon the analogy, a veritable Christmas tree of war. Libations or *spondai* ended the hostilities. Both sides collected their dead and cremated them on the field of battle, after which the ashes were placed in cinerary urns and transported home. The Athenians made ten pyres, one for each of their ten tribes, and then they subsequently conducted a public burial of the cremated remains in Athens (see p. 59). Only rarely, as a signal honour, did they bury their dead on the battlefield, a notable instance being the 192 hoplites who died at the battle of Marathon. A *dekatê* or tithe of the spoils taken from the enemy was dedicated in the victor's temples and sometimes as well, more prestigiously, in a panhellenic sanctuary.

Religious sanctions

Greek religion imposed a number of sanctions upon states at war which were intended to ensure that certain standards of decency were upheld. For the duration of the Olympic Games, and possibly in connection with other international festivals, a sacred truce or *ekecheiria*, literally 'a staying or restraining of one's hands', was in force, which suspended all hostilities. The Spartans declined to lend immediate assistance to the Athenians at the battle of Marathon on the grounds that they were celebrating a festival in honour of Apollo, called the Karneia. This seems a pretty feeble excuse to us, but there is no real reason to doubt that it was genuine. Secondly, an ambassador was placed under the protection of the gods and his person treated as sacrosanct, though one or two cases are known of ambassadors being killed. Thirdly, the defeated side was allowed to return to the battlefield under supervision of the victors in order to collect its dead for burial. Fourthly, the sanctuaries of the defeated had to be left unviolated. The burning of the temples on the Acropolis by the Persians in 480 BC caused such offence to the Athenians that they took an oath to leave them in their ruined condition for ever as a reminder of barbarian savagery, although they rescinded the oath forty years later.

Though war was endemic throughout the Greek world, the standards of behaviour on the battlefield make modern warfare seem unimaginably barbaric by comparison, notwithstanding the rules imposed by the Geneva Convention which are intended to guarantee minimum standards of decency.

Chapter 11
Holy Ground

Sanctuaries varied enormously in size, function and appearance. Some achieved international importance, even though, or rather *because* they were unconnected with any centre of political power, such as those at Delos, Delphi and Olympia. The majority, however, were exclusive to a single community. Those which have left some trace in the archaeological record represent but a tiny fraction of the total that once existed. Pausanias lists seventy sanctuaries in Sparta before he arrives at its acropolis, and Sparta is likely to have had far fewer than, say, Athens. At a site of great antiquity, every minor deity wanted a piece of the action. Virtually every crevice of the north and west slopes of the Acropolis at Athens contained a shrine of some sort, quite apart from the great sanctuaries established on its summit. The basic elements of a sanctuary are uniform throughout the Greek world from early times, as in the case of the Heraion or sanctuary of Hera on Samos, whose origins can be traced to the middle of the eighth century BC (see Fig. 9).

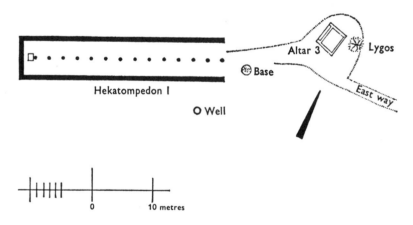

Fig. 9 Sanctuary of Hera on Samos, eighth century BC.

The decision to found a sanctuary

A common motive for founding a sanctuary or *temenos* (literally 'cut off place') was gratitude for deliverance from war, famine or plague. Sanctuaries were frequently established at the prompting of a deity, as in the case of the sanctuary of the goat-footed god Pan in Athens. Herodotus tells us that Pan accosted the Athenian runner Pheidippides before the battle of Marathon with the following words:

> Bear this message to the Athenians. Why don't you pay me cult since I am well-disposed towards you, and have on many occasions already been useful to you and will be so again in the future?
>
> (6.105.2)

After their resounding victory over the Persians, the Athenians duly dedicated a cave to the god on the Acropolis.

Sanctuaries could also be founded by individuals. An inscription from a cave at Vari in southeast Attica reads:

> Archedamos of Thera, the Nymph-raptured one, fitted out this cave at the prompting of the Nymphs.
>
> (*IG* I² 788)

Another inscription, discovered at Phaleron on the south-east coast of Attica, records the founding of a shrine in honour of a river god called Kephisos 'as a thank-offering for the blessing of children' by a woman called Xenokrateia (*IG* II² 4548). Though the shrine was private, the inscription states that 'anyone who wishes to sacrifice may do so on payment of the appropriate fee', indicating that it was available for public use.

The site selected for a sanctuary

The site selected for a sanctuary often had mythological significance. The Erechtheum, which lies just to the north of the Parthenon and which takes its name from a mythical Athenian hero called Erechtheus, stands on the spot where the famous contest between Athena and Poseidon took place to determine which of the two should be the guardian deity of Athens. Within the sanctuary grows the sacred olive tree which Athena caused to grow out of the bare rock as her claim to possession of Attica. Likewise a gap in the north porch marks the place where Poseidon's trident struck the ground, causing a miraculous salt spray – called Erechtheïs – to spurt up out of the ground. The contest for possession of Attica was symbolised by the fact that the Erechtheum was shared between the cults of Athena and Poseidon-Erechtheus.

Many of the most venerable sanctuaries were situated on an acropolis. 'Acropolis' just means 'high *polis*' or the high part of the *polis*. When we hear the word 'acropolis' we tend to think primarily of Athens, but most city-states possessed such a feature. An acropolis had many functions. It was a defensible fortress, the site where the Mycenaean kings had their residences, and holy ground. This three-fold function, military, governmental and religious, in fact conforms to the three-fold role of the Mycenaean kings. As we look at Athens' acropolis today and as it would have looked in antiquity, it is dominated by the Parthenon. But the Parthenon was only one of a number of temples and other religious buildings erected on its artificially levelled platform.

Architectural features of a sanctuary

A sanctuary was simply a piece of consecrated ground. Most were irregular in shape. All had a precise boundary, either in the form of a visible wall (*peribolos*), as in the case of the Athenian Acropolis, or in the form of a few marker stones (*horoi*), as in the case of the sanctuary of Asklepios at Epidaurus. A gateway, known as a propylaea, was not an indispensable requirement, but where it existed it marked the division between secular and religious space in such a way as to enhance the sense of drama upon entering holy ground. The Propylaea on the Acropolis at Athens, although highly ornate, actually functioned as a real gateway, enabling the Acropolis to be locked up.

Temples were usually aligned on an east–west axis. They housed the statue of the deity, as well as the more valuable offerings, including those made of silver and gold. Although temples embodied the finest artistic achievements of the city and functioned as the dwelling place of the deity, no religious ritual was performed inside them. They were therefore by no means indispensable. The Parthenon, which was begun in 448 and dedicated in 436 BC, and which incidentally was paid for by the tribute exacted from Athens' allies, is one of the most perfect buildings ever constructed. Yet when all is said and done it is not much more than a vanity box built to contain – 'show off' might be a better word – the thirty-six foot high chryselephantine (gold and ivory) statue

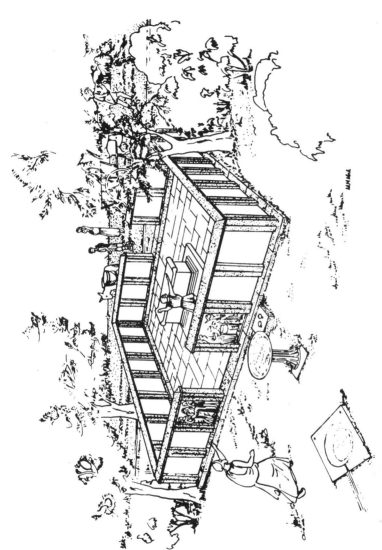

Fig. 10 Altar of the Twelve Gods in Athens, late fifth century BC.

of Athena designed by Pheidias.

The siting of sanctuary buildings does not follow any fixed plan. Even when it would have been easy to achieve perfect axial alignment, it seems not to have been preferred. The essential requirement was an altar or *bômos*, since it was here that the most important devotional act, the sacrifice, was performed. In origin an altar was merely a raised place, but as other structures became more elaborate, so did the altar (see Fig. 10). Few have survived. The most ornate was the altar of Zeus at Pergamum, which was constructed by King Eumenes II (197-159 BC). The great altar of Zeus at Olympia was unique in being simply a pile of ashes composed of former sacrifices.

Many sanctuaries possessed fountain houses, since water is essential in religious ritual. Other optional features included dining rooms or *hestiatoria*, where visiting dignitaries would be entertained at festival time. Healing sanctuaries were provided with *enkoimêtêria* or dormitories for suppliants. International sanctuaries possessed stadia and theatres.

We need to visualise the great sanctuaries as crammed full of votive statuary. One of the largest outdoor statues was that of Athena Promachos, which stood behind the Propylaea on the Athenian Acropolis. Since we know that it was visible to sailors coming from Sounion, the southernmost tip of Attica, it must have been about sixty feet high. Once dedicated, a statue was eternally consecrated to the gods. When the Persians destroyed the Acropolis in 479-80, they also smashed up its marble statues, particularly those depicting young girls (known as *korai*), to which the Athenians subsequently gave ritual burial on the Acropolis. Ironically, we have to thank the Persians for the fact that we know so much about Archaic Athenian sculpture, since the burial of these statues guaranteed their survival.

Sanctuary administration

In charge of a sanctuary was a priest or priestess, whose duties included the supervision of all the ritual conducted within it, the punishment of those who violated the sanctuary regulations, and the maintenance of the buildings in good order. Since most temples were open just a few days each year, their duties were strictly seasonal. Only major sanctuaries provided permanent accommodation. The following inscription outlines the duties of the priest of Amphiaraos in Attica:

Gods! From the onset of winter until spring-ploughing the

priest of Amphiaraos is to go to the sanctuary...with no greater interval than three days between visits. He is to be in residence not less than ten days in each month. He is to require the *neokoros* [temple assistant] to look after the sanctuary in accordance with the law and also to look after those who visit the sanctuary. If anyone commits a crime in the sanctuary, whether he is a stranger or a member of the deme, the priest has authority to fine him up to five drachmas.... Any summons arising from an offence committed in the sanctuary must be issued on the same day. If the defendant does not make restitution, a trial is to be held the next day.

(*IG* VII.235; *SIG*³ 1004; *LSG* 65)

As we have seen (p. 37f.), fear of pollution made it illegal to give birth, have sexual intercourse, die, or bury the dead within a sanctuary. Other prohibitions included pasturing flocks or herds, dumping manure, cutting down wood and lighting fires. Being inviolable and sacrosanct, a sanctuary served as a place of refuge for runaway slaves and others claiming refuge.

Sanctuaries could be leased out like other forms of property. The following inscription dated 306/5 BC describes the terms of the lease of a sanctuary dedicated to the hero Egretes by a religious association of *orgeônes* (i.e. the members of such an association) to a lessee called Diognetos:

Gods! The *orgeônes* lease the sanctuary of Egretes to Diognetos, son of Arkesilos from the deme of Melite, for ten years for a fee of 200 drachmas per year. He is to look after the sanctuary and the buildings erected within it as a sanctuary. Diognetos shall whitewash the walls which need it. He shall construct and arrange whatever else he wants. At the end of the ten-year period he shall take away the woodwork, the roof-tiles and the doors and posts, but he shall not remove the other furnishings. He shall tend the trees growing in the sanctuary. If any tree dies he shall replace it and hand over the same number.

(*SIG*³ 1097; *LSG* 43)

The great age of temple building

Sanctuaries are first detectable from the eighth century onwards and increase dramatically in size over the course of the next two centuries. The votive dedications made during this period are also rich and abundant. The Archaic period was in fact the great age of sanctuaries. Many temples were ruined at the time of the Persian Wars, and as a result considerable re-building was necessary, as at Delphi and Athens. By the beginning of the fourth century, however, many were declining in wealth and importance. The few exceptions include those of Asklepios at Epidaurus, Demeter and Persephone at Eleusis, Apollo Epikourios (Helper) at Bassai, and Athena Alea at Tegea in Arkadia. The decline of the sanctuary in some sense marks the beginning of the decline of the city state, for the two were inextricably bound up together.

Fig. 11   Reconstruction of a terracotta model of a temple from Perachora, c. 700 BC.

Chapter 12
The Great Outdoors

The only Greek state whose festival calendar can be reconstructed in any detail is that of Athens. So numerous were her festivals that one ancient writer whom we call the Old Oligarch mischievously inquired how it was possible to conduct public business when there were so many interruptions (*Constitution of Athens* 3.2). These 'interruptions' were called 'days of release'. Apart from their religious function, festivals also provided 'relaxation from stress', as Pericles (*Thucydides* 2.38) puts it. Athens' religious year began about the summer solstice in late June and consisted of twelve lunar months, each twenty-nine or thirty days in length. There almost certainly existed a set of regulations which set out the city's religious obligations in the lawcode introduced by Solon at the beginning of the sixth century BC. At the end of the fifth century, however, a detailed revision of the festival calendar took place under the supervision of an official transcriber called Nikomachos. The fact that it was necessary to do this reflects the complexity of Athenian religious practices at this date, which were constantly changing as new cults were introduced.

Monthly festivals

The first eight days of the month were devoted to monthly festivals, which mainly took the form of celebrations of divine birthdays. Athena's birthday ('officially' on 28th of the Athenian month, Hekatombaion) was celebrated on the third of every month, Artemis' on the sixth, and Apollo's on the seventh. The first day of the month was called Noumenia or 'New-Moon Day' and was judged to be 'the holiest day of all', as the late writer Plutarch (*Moralia* 828a) tells us.

Agricultural festivals

The largest group of Athens' annual festivals were agricultural in emphasis and were held in honour of Demeter and Dionysos. Most occurred at sowing time, rather than at the harvest, perhaps indicating, as Aristotle (*Nikomachian Ethics* 1160a) suggested, that an agricultural community is not at leisure to engage in festival activity at harvest time. Many of the festivals devoted to Demeter were celebrated in secret by women, no doubt in part because of the close association between women and fertility. As noted (p. 34), they served as a rare occasion when Athenian women could gather together outside the home.

Festivals with a strong agricultural element include the Thesmophoria, a women's festival held in the autumn, when the putrefied remains of pigs which had been thrown into caves were brought up, placed on an altar, and mixed with seed grain; the Oschophoria, a vintage festival which took its name from the fact that two youths of noble families carried *ôschoi* or branches laden with grapes; the Haloa, a women's festival in honour of Demeter celebrated in mid-winter at which pastries in the shape of phalluses were eaten; the Rural Dionysia, when a giant phallus was borne aloft in procession (see p. 32); the Anthesteria or Flower-festival, celebrated in early spring, when wine jars containing newly fermented wine were opened and dedicated to Dionysos; the Thargelia, in honour of Apollo, which took its name from the fact that first fruits or *thargela* in the form of a pot of boiled vegetables were offered to the god, while a human scapegoat was beaten and driven out of the city; and finally, the Pyanopsia, named after *pyanos*, a boiled bean, when olive branches called *eiresionai* laden with wool were borne by children in procession and hung up on the front door of every Athenian home.

Though fertility may have been the chief purpose behind most of the ritual activity performed at these festivals, there are puzzling complications. The Anthesteria, for instance, which was essentially a cheerful three-day festival held in honour of Dionysos, ended on a sombre note with a day of evil omen devoted to the cult of the dead. On this last day, which was known as Chytroi from the fact that *chytroi* or pots of porridge were offered to the dead, ghosts were believed to leave their graves and wander abroad. Precautions against their presence included chewing buckthorn and smearing the doors of one's house with pitch. It has been suggested that two quite separate festivals have somehow merged together, perhaps for no better reason than that they occurred at the same time of the year. Many of the ancient 'explanations' for these various festivals are relatively late, by which time, if not long before, their origins had become shrouded in mystery.

Rites of passage

The second major group comprises festivals, or rites of passage as they are more commonly known today, which had to do with the recognition of age-distinctions. The Apatouria, for instance, was celebrated by hereditary associations called phratries or brotherhoods (p. 31). On its third and final day, newborn infants, youths and newly married wives were officially registered in their phratry. This was called Koureotis or the Day of Hair Shearing, after the ceremony that symbolised the transition to a new status. Formal admission into the religious community took place on the second day of the Anthesteria, known as Choes or Jugs, when Athenian infants in their third or fourth year would be presented with an individual *chous* or jug and experience their first taste of wine. There was also an Athenian festival called the Brauronia held in honour of Artemis of Brauron on the coast of northeast Attica, which included a ritual dance performed by girls aged between seven and eleven who were dressed in saffron robes and 'acted the bear' (whatever that expression means). It is conceivable but by no means certain that the Brauronia in some way symbolised a girl's transition from childhood to puberty.

Festivals for the dead

Thirdly, there were festivals commemorating the dead. We have already mentioned that the last day of the Anthesteria functioned in this way. In addition, there was the Genesia, originally a private festival celebrated on the birthday of a deceased individual, which later became a national day of remembrance for all the dead. Another such festival was the Nemeseia, held at night, which, as its name suggests (from *'nemesis'*, meaning 'vengeance'), was probably intended to placate the angry dead.

One of the most solemn and spectacular events in the Athenian calendar was the annual ceremony for the war dead known as the *taphai* or burials, which took place at the end of the campaigning season in early winter. Thucydides provides the following description of the ritual as performed in the first years of the Peloponnesian War:

> Three days before the ceremony the bones of the dead are brought and put in a tent and people make whatever offerings they wish to the dead. Then there is a funeral procession in which coffins of cypress wood are carried on wagons. There is one coffin for each tribe, which contains the bones of the members of that tribe. One empty bier is decorated and carried in the procession. This is for the missing, whose bodies could not be recovered. Everyone who wishes, both citizens and

foreigners, can join the procession and the women who are
related to the dead are there to make their laments at the tomb....
When the bones have been laid in the earth, a man chosen by
the city for his intellectual gifts and general reputation makes
an appropriate speech in praise of the dead and after the speech
all depart.

(2.34)

The Panathenaia

The most lavish and grandest festivals were those based in the city,
principally the Panathenaia and City Dionysia. The Panathenaia (or
All-Athenian festival) was held annually on the birthday of the city's
patron goddess, Athena. Once every four years it was celebrated with
special pomp, and it is this event which forms the subject of the famous
Parthenon frieze in the British Museum. The festival began with a
procession that proceeded along the Panathenaic Way, so-named after
this festival, towards the Acropolis, its final destination. At its head was
a model of a ship mounted on wheels with an embroidered woollen robe,
known as a *peplos*, rigged to its mast. All elements of the citizen body
took part, including a large military contingent. Resident non-Athenians,
known as metics, also participated as bearers of trays. The rear of the
procession was probably brought up by freed slaves and non-Greeks.

The climax to the whole ceremony was the removal of the goddess'
old *peplos* and its replacement by a new one (see above, p. 33). A
sacrifice of cows then took place and after the goddess had received her
portion, the remainder was distributed to the citizenry in the usual way.
Individual and team events formed part of the competitions at the
accompanying Panathenaic games, including a recitation of the works of
Homer. Prize-winners received amphoras containing olive oil with a
depiction of Athena on one side and the event for which they won it on
the other, inscribed 'One of the prizes from Athens'.

The origins of the Panathenaia are not known but its promotion to
the rank of Athens' premier festival was undoubtedly due in part to
Peisistratos, who was tyrant of Athens around the middle of the sixth
century BC. Clearly it was Peisistratos' intention to make it rival the great
panhellenic festivals, notably the Olympian, Pythian, Nemean and Isth-
mian Games, for which the poet Pindar wrote victory odes. In the
following century the Panathenaia served as an instrument of imperialist
propaganda when Athens passed a law requiring each of her allies to
contribute a cow and a suit of armour as an offering.

The City Dionysia

Peisistratos' further aim of reconciling the urban and rural population of Attica is revealed by his interest in Dionysos, in whose honour the City or Great Dionysia was established. Previously the god had been worshipped only at deme level. This was an occasion when competitions of dramatic and lyric poetry were performed in the theatre of Dionysos on the south slope of the Acropolis. The first victor in the competition for writing tragedy was Thespis (c. 535), from whom our word 'Thespian' derives. In this theatre works were staged that rank among the greatest achievements of Athenian culture, including the tragedies of Aeschylus, Sophocles and Euripides, and the comedies of Aristophanes. It has been estimated that 1,500 people were needed to stage the performances of the City Dionysia with its numerous choruses (nine for tragedy alone). Such a festival presented an opportunity not only to showcase Athens' artistic leadership, but also to demonstrate her political supremacy, since this was when her allies were required to produce their tribute, which was proudly displayed in the theatre to a round of applause from the audience. The Athenians, as well as their gods, certainly got their money's worth. Dramatic performances also took place at a festival called the Lenaea, likewise held in honour of Dionysos, from which, however, foreigners were excluded (cf. Aristophanes, *Acharnians* 502-5).

Chapter 13
'Ars Non Gratia Artis'

The study of Greek art is inseparable from the study of Greek religion because virtually all of it, whatever its function, had a religious significance. There was precious little art for art's sake in the Greek world, at least as far as the major arts were concerned. The most common word for an art object is '*agalma*', which means 'a thing of joy'. '*Agalma*' indicates that an art object was intended to give pleasure to the gods, to the living, and, to the extent that they possessed sentience, to the dead. The fullest expression of the community's desire to give pleasure to its gods is embodied in the temple, whose pediments, metopes and friezes provided a space for compositions which mainly illustrated episodes from the lives of the gods, although the great frieze which ran around the outer wall of the Parthenon depicted the celebration of the Panathenaia (see p. 60). Free-standing statues in the form of cult statues, statues dedicated to a god in fulfilment of a vow, and honorific statues were either erected in sanctuaries or beside graves. They were not exhibited in museums because museums did not exist. Nor until the late fourth century were they displayed in private houses because there were no private collectors.

The Greeks believed that some statues were invested with a life of their own. This is demonstrated by an amusing anecdote told by Pausanias about an athlete called Theagenes of Thasos who won no fewer than 1,400 crowns for his athletic prowess (6.11.5-8). When Theagenes died, his rival, who had been constantly beaten by him in contests, took his revenge by flogging the bronze statue which had been erected in his honour, 'as if it were Theagenes himself he was maltreating'. Eventually the statue got fed up and toppled over, thereby crushing his tormentor to death. All this may sound far-fetched, but there's more to follow. The dead man's sons now proceeded to prosecute the statue for murder. After it had been found guilty, it was dumped in the sea in accordance with the lawcode of Draco 'who banished even lifeless things if they had killed anyone by falling on top of him'. A famine followed and when the Thasians consulted the Delphic Oracle, they were told that they must recall the exiled Theagenes. Eventually they recovered his statue and

re-dedicated it, whereupon the famine ceased. In order to comes to terms
with the Greek notion that a statue of a god or hero possesses a life of its
own, it may help us to bear in mind that both the Roman Catholic and
Orthodox Churches lay great emphasis upon the power of images to work
miracles.

Cult statues

A cult statue of a deity or hero was an object of worship, rather like the
golden calf which the children of Israel worship at Mount Sinai in
Exodus. The assumption behind this practice is, of course, that the
man-made object isn't an inanimate piece of wood or stone at all but in
a very real sense divine. A cult statue was not, however, just *any* statue
of a deity or hero. It was usually a very old and often somewhat
nondescript object, like the olive-wood statue of Athena Polias housed
on the Acropolis which Pausanias describes as 'the holiest thing there
is' (1.26.6). It was this statue, believed to have fallen out of the sky, which
was draped in the embroidered *peplos* that was presented to Athena at
the Panathenaia (see p. 60). There were other statues of Athena on the
Acropolis, such as the great chryselephantine statue of Athena Parthenos
inside the Parthenon. This was much larger and far more spectacular, but
it wasn't particularly holy and, so far as we know, it wasn't the focus of
any ritual activity.

Votive offerings

Statues in the form of votive offerings, the chief currency, so to speak,
of Greek religion, abounded. A seventh-century statuette dedicated to
Apollo by a certain Mantiklos carries the following message to the god,
which is engraved on its thigh: 'Mantiklos offers me as a tithe to
silver-bowed Apollo. You, Phoibos, give me something pleasing in
return.' Votive statuary ranged in size from tiny figurines to over-lifesize
figures. They either represented the donor, the deity or some go-
between.

One of the earliest full-scale figures in Greek art is a dedication to
Artemis of Delos by a woman from Naxos called Nikandre, which was
carved about the middle of the seventh century BC (see Fig. 12). Among
the finest monuments of Archaic art are the magnificent series of
maidens (*korai*) from the Athenian Acropolis, three dozen in all, which
were dedicated to Athena (c. 560-480 BC). As their dress indicates, this
type of statue originated in Ionia and spread thence to Attica. A prototype

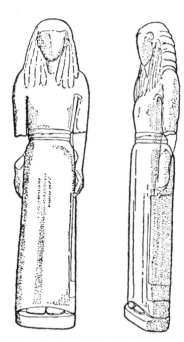

Fig. 12 Votive offering of Nikandre the Naxian.

Fig. 13 Group of statues by Geneleos, c. 560.

for their design is a set of six marble statues which were carved by an artist called Geneleos in c. 560 BC for the sanctuary of Hera on Samos (Fig. 13).

After a victory in battle, states dedicated statues which were paid for from the tithe given to the gods (see p. 48). One such was the bronze statue of Athena Promachos which stood on the Acropolis, paid from the spoils of Marathon. Another, dedicated at Delphi and commemorating the same victory, consisted of a group of thirteen bronze statues, including those of Athena, Apollo, the dead Athenian general Miltiades who had been the architect of the Athenian victory, and Athens' ten tribal heroes.

Statues of the living

Until the Hellenistic period (conventionally dated from the death of Alexander the Great in 323 BC) honorific statues were erected almost exclusively to victorious athletes and were funded by the community to which the victor belonged. Inasmuch as the majority were erected in sanctuaries as a kind of thank-offering for the athletic prowess of the victor, they, too, are invested with a religious significance. It is a measure of the importance that attached to athletic activity in the Greek world that this was the principal activity that was so honoured. With a few notable exceptions, such as Kresilas' famous statue of the statesman Pericles, it was not until the Hellenistic period that the practice of honouring non-athletes with statues became common. One of the most famous surviving examples is the Delphic Charioteer, which was originally part of a bronze four-horse chariot group dedicated by a certain Polyzelos, tyrant of Gela in Sicily, who owned the team, commemorating his victory in 474 BC.

Statues of the dead

In the sixth century BC it was fashionable for Athenian aristocrats to erect free-standing statues of their dead marking the spot where they were buried, which in this period was usually on the family estate. There can be little doubt that these statues served in part to advertise the family's wealth and prestige. Designated *kouroi* (youths) by art historians, they conventionally depict a young man at the peak of his physical accomplishment, naked and striding confidently forward. *Kouroi* are also found in sanctuaries of Apollo. In fact if we do not know the find-spot, it is impossible to determine whether they were dedicated to the dead or to Apollo. *Korai* may also have occasionally served as funerary markers.

Kouroi were banned around 480 BC, evidently because they were regarded as aggressive symbols of aristocratic pomp and privilege, and for over half a century no permanent grave-markers were erected in Athens. The Classical series begins around 430 BC, when it became customary to erect marble monuments with pediments resembling miniature temples called *naïskoi*. Inside the *naïskos* the deceased are depicted in the company of their relatives, either saying farewell in this world or greeting one another in the world to come. Legislation was introduced in the final decades of the fourth century banning the series and thereafter only the simplest forms of grave-markers were erected (Fig. 15; see p. 71).

Chapter 14
'From Here to There'

'From here to there' is a translation of a common Greek expression for the journey that the dead must take from this world to the next. The journey was facilitated by the relatives of the deceased, whose duty was to ensure that the transfer was effected as rapidly and efficiently as possible. Whatever it did for the deceased, however, we should not ignore the fact that a costly, elaborate and well-attended funeral provided a perfect vehicle for the conspicuous display of family wealth, power and prestige.

The importance of burial

The necessity of conducting burial rites, and the corresponding insult to human dignity if they be omitted, is frequently alluded to in literature, notably in Sophocles' *Antigone*, whose heroine, though forbidden to bury her brother Polyneikes because he is a traitor, is caught sprinkling earth over his corpse. In defence of her action she declares that the claims of the dead come under the heading of the 'unwritten laws', which are of such force that they cannot be overridden by an edict of man (453-5). Such was the vital importance of burial and the subsequent rituals conducted at regular intervals on behalf of the dead that childless Athenians frequently adopted an heir in order to ensure that their mortal remains received proper attention. The performance of these rites is frequently adduced in lawsuits involving cases of disputed adoption to prove that the claimant had (or did not have) genuine kinship with the deceased, as in this example:

> I, the adopted son, with the aid of my wife…tended Menekles while he was alive. When he died, I buried him in a manner fitting both to him and myself and set up a fine monument to him and performed the customary rituals on the ninth day and all the other required rituals at the tomb in the finest way I could.
>
> (Isaeus, *On the Estate of Menekles* 2.36)

The funeral

A Greek funeral was a three-act drama consisting of the laying out or
prothesis of the body, the funeral cortège or *ekphora* (carrying out), and
the interment. It was an entirely domestic affair from which priests were
debarred because of their need to remain ritually pure. We only rarely
hear of undertakers and it is evident that the relatives of the deceased
usually disposed of the corpse without any professional assistance.

Upon decease, the corpse's eyes and mouth were closed. The
well-known custom of placing a small coin known as an obol in the
mouth as payment to Charon, the ferryman of the dead, was a late
innovation and by no means universally upheld. To prevent the unsightly
sagging of the lower jaw, a chin-strap was tied around the head. The body
was washed and dressed and then laid out on a couch with the feet facing
towards the door – a practice, incidentally, which appears to be well-nigh
universal and which has given rise to the English expression 'to carry
out feet first'. We know a great deal about the *prothesis*, which was
handled exclusively by women, because it is the subject of a number of
paintings on *loutrophoroi*, a type of vase which was used for the nuptial
bath (see p. 30).

Representations of the second act, the *ekphora*, are much fewer,
but we gain some impression of what the ceremony involved from the
following regulations which were passed by the phratry of the Labyads
at Delphi in c. 400 BC outlawing certain practices that were obviously
very popular:

> The corpse shall be transported covered up and in silence.
> There shall be no stopping on the way, and no lamentations
> outside the house before reaching the grave. In the case of the
> previous dead, there shall be no dirge or lamentation over their
> tombs. Everyone shall go straight back home, apart from those
> who share the same hearth as the deceased, together with
> paternal uncles, parents-in-law, descendants and sons-in-law.
>
> (*LGS* 77 = *SIG*³ 1220)

What happened during the final act of the drama, the interment
itself, we know least about. We do not even know whether there existed
a standard burial service with a customary form of words delivered at
the graveside, as the body or cinerary urn containing the ashes was being
interred. Homer's description of the cremation of Hector with which the

Iliad ends describes a heroic-style Greek burial:

> For nine days they gathered an immeasurable amount of wood, but when the tenth day dawned, giving light to mortals, they carried out bold Hector, shedding tears, and placed his corpse on the top of the pyre, and set light to it.... And when they had all gathered together, first they quenched the fire with flaming wine as far as the fire had reached. Hector's brothers and companions gathered up the whitened bones, mourning and shedding big tears down their cheeks. They placed the bones in a golden casket, which they covered with soft purple robes. Then they straightway laid it in a hollow grave, which they covered with large stones packed close together.... When they had piled the mound, they returned...and enjoyed a glorious feast in the palace of King Priam, nurtured by Zeus.
>
> (24.784-803)

Both cremation and inhumation were practised by the Greeks at various times in their history, often concurrently and with no evident distinction in beliefs concerning the fate of the deceased.

In Classical Athens rites were also performed at the tomb on the third, ninth and thirtieth days after the burial. Only when these had been properly discharged could the relatives take comfort from the fact that they had done everything they could to effect the transfer of the deceased 'from here to there'.

Place of burial

In early times in Athens burial was permitted inside the city, but around 500 BC this practice was forbidden. Henceforth the dead were usually interred alongside major thoroughfares outside the city walls, though some were buried on private estates. The preferred area was the Kerameikos or Potters' Quarter on the west side of Athens beside the great Dipylon Gate. Here, too, the Athenians buried their war dead in communal graves known as *polyandreia*. The most lavish and ostentatious private graves possessed a retaining wall on three of their four sides (see Fig. 14). Though ease of access was probably the primary motive for burying alongside a major thoroughfare, a plot beside a well-frequented road was also a marvellous advertisement for the family's wealth and prestige. Many plots resemble a fortress, their apparent intention being not merely to impress but also to intimidate potential tomb robbers. One

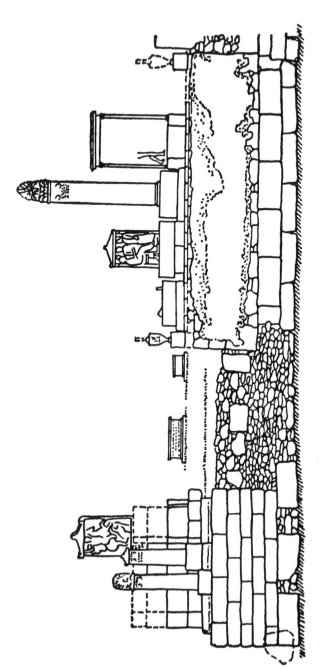

Fig. 14 Family graves in the Kerameikos, Athens.

such family tomb cost 5,000 drachmas – and that at a time when a day's pay for a rower in the fleet was a single drachma. The most lavish that has so far come to light was erected by two metics in c. 330 BC to the south of Athens, and it is more like a temple than a tomb. The expense lavished on such structures had got so out of hand by this point that in 317 BC Demetrios of Phaleron introduced legislation banning all but the simplest form of grave-markers (see Fig. 15).

Fig. 15   Hellenistic grave-marker from Athens. A so-called *kioniskos* (little column) with ivy wreath in low relief, inscribed 'Hieronymos'.

Grave gifts

The quality of gifts placed in the grave declined markedly over the centuries. In the Geometric period (i.e. ninth-eighth centuries BC), the dead were often buried with gold jewellery, weapons and other metal objects (see Fig. 16), whereas in the succeeding Archaic period they were usually provided with little more than a cup or a bowl. In fifth-century Athens the commonest offering was a white-ground *lêkythos* or oil-flask often manufactured with a solid clay bottom so that only a very small amount of oil was necessary to fill it. Evidently the dead did not mind being 'cheated'! By the beginning of the fourth century, however, the popularity of *lêkythoi* had so declined that in one of Aristophanes' plays a youth pokes fun at an old woman for having as her lover a geriatric 'who paints *lêkythoi* for the dead' (*Women in Assembly* 996). One of the most poignant reminders of mortality is provided by jugs known as *choes*, which were deposited in the graves of very young children and illustrated with touching scenes from childhood (see p. 59).

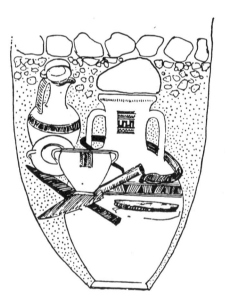

Fig. 16 Cremation burial in the Athenian Agora. A bent sword is wrapped around the neck of the amphora, which contains the ashes of the deceased.

The cult of the tomb

Even when rites of burial had been accomplished, the deceased, at least
in the Classical period, continued to enjoy a lively relationship with their
surviving relatives, who were expected to take an active interest in their
welfare by paying visits to the grave on a regular basis. The belief that
the dead needed sustenance survived throughout Greek history. In earlier
times the most common victims offered to the dead were sheep and oxen.
In fifth-century Athens animal offerings were largely replaced by cake,
wine and olive oil. It also became a common practice in this period to
tie brightly-coloured sashes around the shaft of the grave-marker. We
know a great deal about the Athenian cult of the tomb because it is the
most frequently depicted scene on the white-ground *lêkythoi* mentioned
above. These scenes indicate that those who visited the tomb, like those
who performed the *prothesis*, were predominantly women (see p. 35).

Chapter 15
The Dead

The dead, like the living, are differentiated, and Greek funerary practices were substantially modified in the case of those who died in their prime, the unburied dead, victims of murder, suicides, heroes, and other special groups. We will begin, however, by looking at beliefs surrounding the ordinary dead.

The ordinary dead

The Homeric dead are truly pathetic in their helplessness, inhabiting draughty, echoing halls, deprived of their wits, desperate for the latest news, and flitting purposely about uttering bat-like noises (*Odyssey* 24.5ff.). Much the same seems to be true of them throughout Greek history. The cult of the tomb is premised on the assumption that the living can benefit the dead by providing them with food and drink, upon which the dead are apparently dependent for their general well-being. Incidentally, the precise relationship between the living body and the *psychê* (spirit of the dead) is unclear, since the latter is referred to only in connection with the dead.

But though powerless in themselves, the dead had access to the infernal powers, notably Hades (Aïdoneus) and Persephone (see p. 7). Thus from the late fifth century onwards it became a custom to place folded lead plaques known as *katadesmoi* or 'things for binding down' in graves. These were inscribed with curses bearing the name of the person to be 'bound down', in the belief that the dead would act as messengers to the chthonic gods. A regularly repeated formula runs, 'I bind down the eyes, the mouth, the *psychê*, the sanity, the arms, the legs, of so-and-so.' In order to reach the dead, these plaques were usually pierced with a nail which 'cancelled' them for use by the living, like other objects dispatched to the underworld (see Fig. 17). We also find small lead figures with their arms bound behind their back.

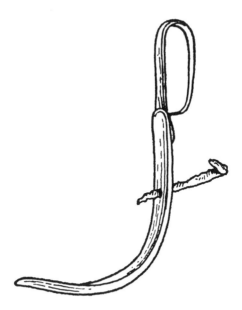

Fig. 17 Strigil (or scraper used by athletes) 'cancelled' (i.e. reserved for the dead) by iron nail.

The untimely dead

Infants who died in the first years of their life probably received abbreviated funerary rites. The Greeks also felt special sympathy towards those who died at a marriageable age but were unmarried. As if to emphasise the bitterness of their fate, a special marker known as a *loutrophoros* was placed over their graves resembling the type of vase which was used for the ritual bath accompanying the marriage ceremony (see p. 68). The dead in both these categories would have been very numerous in a society where infant mortality was high and where a large percentage of the population failed to survive adolescence.

The murdered dead

Lawcourt speeches frequently urge the jury to render assistance to the dead as if they were unable to look after their own interests (e.g. Lysias 12.99). But that is not true of all the dead. Victims of murder were thought of as vengeful and malignant, as we learn from the grisly practice of *maschalismos*, according to which the murderer sought to neutralise their anger by cutting off their extremities or *maschalismata*, i.e. hands and feet (cf. Sophocles, *Electra* 445).

The heroic dead

In the last quarter of the eighth century BC the Greeks began making offerings in connection with Bronze Age, i.e. Mycenaean, tombs. Evidently these tombs had come to light either accidentally or as the result of a deliberate archaeological search, and their contents were attributed to famous heroes like Agamemnon, Menelaus, Ajax, Achilles and so forth. At Mycenae, for instance, there was a cult of Agamemnon and at Sparta a cult of Menelaus and Helen. There can be little doubt that the inspiration for the worship of heroes, like that of the Olympians, derived partly from epic poetry, although, paradoxically, Homer never alludes to the worship of heroes or indeed to tomb cult. In his poems '*hêrôs*' means little more than 'man'. A hero's services could be invoked most effectively by animal sacrifice. To enable the blood to reach the hero directly, a clay pipe was sometimes inserted into his grave. The model for invoking a hero is the sacrifice of a black ram and black sheep which Odysseus performs at the beginning of *Odyssey* 11, though he actually performs it on behalf of the ordinary dead.

Comparisons are often made between the cult of heroes and the cult of saints. But though points of contact do exist, the analogy is fundamentally misleading. The most important distinction between a saint and a hero is that the latter achieves heroic status not because of his saintliness or love of God but because he is, to put it in the simplest possible terms, too big for human life. The acts which he performs during his lifetime, whether voluntary or involuntary, are unlike anything that lesser mortals experience. And that, as usual in Greek religion, includes acts of both wickedness and goodness. Oedipus becomes a hero at the end of his life because he has committed two of the most awful crimes imaginable. He has killed his father and married his mother. His experience is thus unlike that of any other human being. Other heroes, like Theseus and Herakles, were heroised because they rid the world of monsters. Hero-cults were also associated with the mythical founders of various communities. Pelops, for instance, was worshipped in part because he was believed to be the founder of the Peloponnese or 'island of Pelops'. In Athens there existed a cult of ten Eponymous heroes, who gave their names to the ten Athenian tribes (see Fig. 18). Exceptionally,

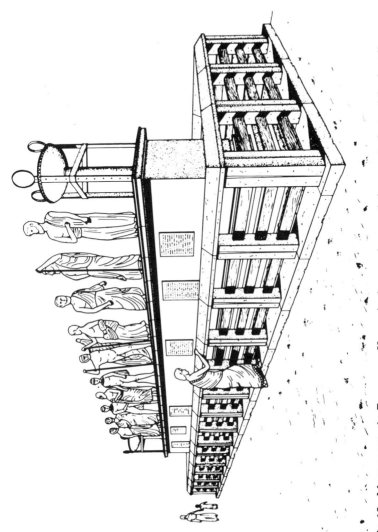

Fig. 18   Monument to the Eponymous Heroes, i.e. heroes who gave their names to the ten Athenian tribes.

too, the war dead were heroised, as in the case of the Athenians who died at Marathon in 490 BC and the Greeks who died at Plataia in 479. (It has been suggested that the famous cavalcade of horsemen on the frieze running around the outer wall of the Parthenon is intended to represent the Marathonian dead.) In the Hellenistic period heroisation became an almost routine occurrence, being awarded to civic benefactors for acts of generosity. But by this time it had ceased to be a lively expression of belief.

The principal theory behind hero-cult was that a hero's physical remains were powerful. How significant the cult was may be judged from the fact that in the mid-sixth century, when Sparta was attempting to extend her control over the northeast Peloponnese, she received an oracle recommending that she retrieve the bones of Orestes. She duly exhumed a coffin at Tegea containing a body seven cubits in length (i.e. about twelve or thirteen feet) and brought it back home. The bones did the trick and Sparta won the war (Herodotus 1.67-8). Likewise a *phasma* or ghost of the Athenian hero Theseus was observed fighting at the battle of Marathon (Plutarch, *Life of Theseus* 35.5). Clearly there is *some* parallel with the cult of saints, whose bones are also invested with supernatural power. But whereas the cult of saints deals in parts of the saint's body, the cult of heroes required that the entire body be intact, although there must have been occasions when it was not fully recoverable. A hero's remains were powerful only in the vicinity of the grave and particularly as a protection against enemy attack. In Sophocles' *Oedipus at Kolonos* Oedipus promises that his body will assist Athens in any future war that she has with Thebes (616-23). Compared with the Olympian deities, therefore, the assistance which heroes offered was both localised and limited.

Chapter 16
The Afterlife

The Greeks did not believe in only one type of afterlife. Though the dominant belief was in Hades, the home of the undifferentiated dead, the Isles of the Blest, Elysion, the transformation of the dead into stars, their absorption into the upper atmosphere, and re-incarnation are just some of the other possibilities. There are also the beliefs associated with the Eleusinian Mysteries and certain 'fringe' sects, which will be discussed in chapters 17 and 18.

Hades

The earliest description of Aïdes, the unseeing or unseen place, to give it its proper epic form, is provided by Homer, who in *Odyssey* 11 describes Odysseus having converse with the dead in order to learn about the situation back at home on Ithaca. Achilles sums up the Greek attitude towards Hades when he says 'I'd rather be a day labourer on earth working for a man of little property than lord of all the hosts of the dead' (11.489-91). Hardly any Greek looked forward to being dead – or at least not because he expected a better life in the world below. The principal activities of the Homeric dead appear to be gossip, sententious moralising and self-indulgent regret (e.g. *Odyssey* 24.20ff.).

Notwithstanding the fact that Hades held few attractions, entry to it was critical for the peace of mind and welfare of the deceased. That, in part, was why burial was so important. When Achilles delays burying Patroklos because he is unable to detach himself from his friend, the latter's ghost appears to him in his sleep and says, 'Bury me as soon as possible so that I can pass through the gates of Hades' (*Iliad* 23.71). It is for the same reason that a young man called Elpenor, who falls from the roof of Circe's palace, requests burial from Odysseus when the latter summons the spirits of the dead by blood sacrifice (*Odyssey* 11.51-82). However draughty and cheerless it may have been, Hades was the home, quite literally, of the dead. Burial was important for sentimental reasons as well. Whether or not we believe in the world to come, it is not easy to contemplate our nearest and dearest lying unburied. People who committed crimes against the state were denied burial not only because such a punishment deprived their relatives of the opportunity to mourn their deaths publicly, but also because it denied the dead access to the underworld. That is the central issue in Sophocles' *Antigone* (see p. 67). Others who might be denied access to Hades were suicides and murderers. Their fate is not altogether clear but it is obvious that they are unhappy as a result of their outlawed condition.

Hades has its own bureaucracy. Hermes Psychopompos, for instance, is conductor of the dead, equipped with a wand or *rhabdos* with which he touches the eyes of the dead in order to wake them up for their journey to Hades. He appears to be a fairly friendly figure. On an Athenian *lêkythos* he is depicted as biding his time while the woman he has come to escort makes up in a mirror, evidently in order to make a good impression down below. Charon, the ferryman of the dead, was probably imported into Greece from the Near East or Egypt. We encounter two kinds of Charons in Greek art, stern Charons and kindly Charons, but it is characteristic of Greek belief that the latter predominate. We even encounter a comic Charon in Aristophanes' *Frogs*. Upon arrival at the gates of Hades, the dead encounter the multi-headed dog Cerberus (there's disagreement as to the exact number of heads), who makes sure they do not try to escape just in case they are having second thoughts. And finally, there is the lord of the dead, Hades/Aïdoneus, known also as Dis and Pluto, and his ever-youthful bride Persephone.

If Hades was joyless it also held few terrors, and that goes equally for the place as for the people who ran it. The region is rarely represented in Greek art, for reasons that we can only speculate about. An exception was a lost painting by the fifth-century artist Polygnotos (Pausanias 10.28-31). Did the Greeks shun such images out of loathing and disgust for the region, out of inability to depict it convincingly, or out of plain disinterest? *Lêkythoi* rarely depict Hermes and Charon and never the region beyond the Styx. Apart from *Odyssey* 11, the only other detailed description of Hades is to be found in Aristophanes' *Frogs*, where Dionysos goes to the underworld in search of Euripides, though on arrival he decides to retrieve his predecessor Aeschylus instead. There are also brief descriptions of Hades on gold leaves previously attributed by scholars to Orphism, but now thought to be connected with Pythagoreanism or the Dionysian Mysteries.

Post-mortem rewards and punishments

The concept of Heaven and Hell is largely absent from Greek eschatology.

Although we encounter a judge called Minos in the *Odyssey*, his role is to decide lawsuits between the litigious dead, not to discriminate between the saved and the damned (11.568-70). It is true that Menelaos, king of Sparta, is told that he is not going to die but be taken to the Elysian fields 'where life is easiest for men' (4.565). The reason, however, is not because he is virtuous or god-fearing, but because, being the husband of Helen, he is the son-in-law of Zeus. (An eternity in the Elysian Fields may be considered a small reward for his wife's flagrant infidelity!) We also hear of the Isles of the Blest, which is where the race of heroes live on, a sort of Valhalla for brave warriors. Post-mortem punishment was largely reserved for those who had grievously offended the gods, like Tantalos, who served up his son Pelops in a stew in order to see if they would be so foolish as to eat human flesh. Other terrible criminals include Ixion, who was tied to a burning wheel which rotated constantly, and Sisyphos, who was condemned to roll an enormous rock eternally uphill.

Philosophers like Plato also advanced the theory that one's behaviour in this world determined one's fate in the next, as is hinted at in the following comment which he puts into the mouth of the elderly Kephalos:

> When a man gets near to the end of his life, he becomes subject
> to fear and anxiety about what lies ahead. The stories told about
> people in Hades, that if you commit crimes on earth you must
> pay for them down below, although they were ridiculed for a
> while, now begin to disturb a man's *psychê* with the possibility
> that they might be true.
>
> (*Republic* 1.330d-e)

But whether Kephalos speaks for the majority we do not know. Belief in post-mortem punishments and rewards also seems to have been held by the Orphics, as we shall see in chapter 18.

Becoming a star or pure air

Celestial transformation, that is, the conversion of the dead into stars, as in the case of Castor and Pollux, the heavenly twins, or their conversion into aither or pure air, seems to have been reserved as a reward. An epitaph on the Athenian war dead at the siege of Potidaia (432-429 BC) reads, 'The moist aither received their *psychai*, but earth their bodies' (*IG* I² 945).

Transmigration of souls

Belief in the transmigration of the soul from one body to another at the moment of death (*metempsychôsis*) is propounded at some length in Plato's *Phaedo* (107d-108c) and in other dialogues. The concept probably entered Greece from Egypt and was advanced by Pythagoras, who even claimed that he could remember his previous incarnations. It is another idea that is largely confined to philosophy, and by no means all philosophers at that. Xenophanes of Kolophon (see ch. 20), for instance, told the following facetious anecdote about Pythagoras:

> They say that he was once passing by when a puppy was being whipped. Taking pity on the animal, Pythagoras said, 'Stop. Don't beat it. It is the *psychê* of my friend, whom I recognised when I heard him speaking.'
>
> (*DK* 21 fr. 7)

Chapter 17
Mysteries

We turn next to an aspect of Greek religion that is by definition anything but clear in outline. I say 'by definition' because the Greek word for it is *mystêrion*, our word 'mystery', which means literally 'a ceremony or place of initiation'. A mystery religion is one which required its devotees to go through a rite of initiation. I shall deal here exclusively with the Eleusinian Mysteries, which were devoted to the worship of Demeter, her daughter Persephone (also known simply as Kore, 'Daughter'), and an Eleusinian hero called Triptolemos, although I would emphasise that the Mysteries celebrated at Eleusis are just one manifestation – admittedly *the* most important and best documented manifestation – of a number of mystery religions that were popular throughout the Greek world.

The Eleusinian Mysteries were celebrated twice a year, the Lesser in March and the Greater in September. Women, non-citizens and slaves were all permitted to undergo initiation. Only murderers and those who could not speak Greek were excluded. There were three stages of initiation: preliminary initiation into the Lesser Mysteries, initiation proper (*teletê*) into the Greater Mysteries, and higher initiation (*epopteia*) for those who were already *mystai* or initiates.

Eleusis

Eleusis, the home of the Mysteries, is situated on the Attic coast some 13 miles west of Athens. In antiquity the township possessed rich agricultural land known as the Rarian field where, according to legend, corn was first said to have been sown by Triptolemos. At some point in history, probably around 600 BC, control of Eleusis passed into the hands of the Athenian state, though the Mysteries never became exclusive to Athens. The sanctuary reached the height of its importance in the fourth century BC and declined thereafter, although it underwent something of a revival in the second century AD. In total, the Mysteries were celebrated at Eleusis for over one thousand years. It is clear, too, that for a time they presented a serious rival to Christianity, because Christian graffiti deface many of the monuments and because Christian writers consistently suggest that the rituals connected with the sanctuary were disgusting and obscene. Clement of Alexandria, for instance, a writer who flourished in the second half of the second century AD, refers to murder, indecency, sex and criminality as part of what went on behind closed doors.

Eleusinian secrecy

The unknown author of the 'Homeric' *Hymn to Demeter*, which is believed to be based on ritual practices associated with the Eleusinian Mysteries, states (476): 'To the kings of Eleusis Demeter showed the conduct of her rites and taught them her mysteries, awful mysteries which no one can transgress or utter.' The rites were so secret in fact that the Athenian state imposed the death penalty on anyone who was convicted of divulging them. The poet Aeschylus is said to have nearly been executed under this charge. The politician Alkibiades was condemned *in absentia* for having burlesqued the Eleusinian Mysteries. Aristophanes in the *Frogs*, which has a chorus of initiates, describes the procession in a fanciful way but divulges none of the secrets. The traveller Pausanias took their secrets so seriously that he actually refrained from mentioning the buildings in the sanctuary, claiming that he was prevented from so doing 'by a vision in a dream'. Christian writers provide some account of the Mysteries but their testimonies cannot be trusted, firstly because they are partisan and secondly because they confuse the Eleusinian Mysteries with Orphic rites (see ch. 18). The following remarks by Tertullian, who was virulently opposed to all pagan rites, are typical:

> Even the celebrated Eleusinia, that heresy of Attic superstition, is a shameful thing about which they keep quiet. In fact they impose torture before they certify the admission of an initiate. They start the *epoptai* off five years before so that they may build up their expectations by withholding knowledge and so that they may seem to reveal something of a grandeur equivalent to the greed which they have heaped up. Following this there is an obligation of silence. This is kept assiduously because it is learned at a later stage. However, the entire godhead in the innermost sanctuary, the entire source of breathless adulation in the *epoptai*, the entire secret token of their tongues, is revealed to be – an image of the male organ!
>
> (*Against the Valentinians* 1)

The ritual as we know it

It follows from all this that what we know about the Eleusinian Mysteries is largely confined to certain public actions. We can therefore only guess at the 'spiritual' meaning of the Mysteries. We do know, however, that they were centrally concerned with the afterlife, as is suggested by the myth of the rape of Persephone. The location for the myth is Eleusis itself and it tells the story of how Persephone was forced to wed the king of the underworld. In consequence she had to spend one third of all eternity in his kingdom, though she was permitted to spend the other two-thirds on Mount Olympus in the company of her mother Demeter.

The Greater Mysteries opened with a procession of sacred objects known as *hiera* which were carried in baskets from the Telesterion or Hall of Initiation in Eleusis to Athens, where they lodged temporarily in a building known as the Eleusinion. A proclamation was made by a sacred herald, inviting all Greeks to attend and at the same time warning murderers and non-Greek speakers to keep away. Each person undergoing initiation then went down to the Piraeus, the port of Athens, with a small pig and bathed themselves and their pig in the sea. The pigs were subsequently sacrificed to the Two Goddesses. (You will recall that pigs are the most potent purifiers.) The sacred objects were then conveyed back to Eleusis in a procession to the accompaniment of hymns that were chanted in honour of an obscure deity called Iakchos. The procession set out in the afternoon and arrived in Eleusis at sunset. It was headed by a chariot bearing a statue of Iakchos. At a certain point in the journey, when the procession came to a bridge close to the deme of Eleusis, the *mystai* were jeered at by the people of Eleusis. (Incidentally, ritual abuse plays a significant part in many religious rites, such as a Roman triumph.) This return to Eleusis was in a sense the climax of the public festival. When the procession arrived at the sanctuary the *hiera* were then handed over to the *hierophant* or 'shower of sacred things', who was the chief priest.

The initiation ceremony was performed in the Telesterion, a building containing six rows of seven columns without any windows which was lit by a small aperture in the centre of the roof. At its maximum this held about 3,000 people. What happened inside is a real mystery. It is tempting to suppose that initiates were worked up into a heightened state of consciousness partly induced by fasting – we know for a fact that they did fast – and that in the mysterious darkness of the Telesterion apparitions paraded before them, since we hear of *legomena* (things said), *drômena* (things done) and *deiknymena* (things shown). The *deiknymena* may have taken the form of a liturgical drama, conceivably a re-enactment of the abduction of Persephone by Pluto. But other interpretations and reconstructions are possible, and finally we have to admit our ignorance. A church father called Hippolytos of Rome said that the *hierophant* displayed an ear of cut wheat at the climax of the ceremony. Clement of Alexandria gives the following statement as the 'watchword' or 'sacred formula' (*synthema*) of the Mysteries:

> I have fasted, I have drunk the *kykeion* [a ritual drink made of pulse, pennyroyal and water], I have taken from the *kistê* [a sacred basket], worked, deposited [it] into the *kalathos* [another type of basket] and out of the *kalathos* into the *kistê*.
>
> (*Protreptikos* 2.21.2)

Clement (who doesn't say what the 'it' is) then goes on to enumerate the contents of the *kistê*, which include sesame cakes, cakes shaped like pyramids and balls, lumps of salt, a serpent, pomegranates, sprigs of fig, fennel and ivy, cheese-cakes and poppies. 'These', he declares scornfully, 'are their sanctities!' One cannot help reflecting that a Roman Catholic mass would probably appear equally baffling to someone who knew nothing about its significance.

The most important literary evidence for what transpired at the Mysteries is much earlier. Towards the conclusion of the 'Homeric' *Hymn to Demeter* we read:

> Prosperous is he among men who has seen these things; but he who is uninitiated and has no part in the sacred things (*hiera*), never has the lot of a like destiny once he has perished and gone beneath the misty darkness.
>
> (480-2)

Identical in tone is this fragment from a Pindaric dirge:

> Prosperous is he who having seen these things passes below the earth. He knows the end of life and its god-given beginning [or 'principle', *archê*].
>
> (fr. 121 *OCT*)

What this seems to imply is that the Eleusinian Mysteries promised eternal bliss purely on ritualistic grounds. Did the Mysteries also demand a certain quality of life from their initiates or was initiation itself enough? Certainly Diogenes the Cynic did not believe that ethical considerations played any part in determining a person's destiny in the next life on the basis of what he knew about the Mysteries, for he sneeringly remarked, 'What! Do you mean that Pataikion the thief will have a better lot after death than Epaminondas because he has been initiated?' (Plutarch, *Moralia* 21f.).

Correspondences with Christianity

Whatever the answer to that question, scholars have, rightly in my view, seen correspondences between Christianity and the Eleusinian Mysteries. I would sum these up as follows:

1. Both promise blessedness in the world to come, especially to those in the lower ranks of society;
2. Both make a universal appeal – or at least one that is not confined by the borders of the Greek city state;
3. The mythology of both is 'family-centred', N.B. the central position of mother and child;
4. The death of the central figure is resolved by resurrection;
5. Non-initiates, like sinners, are assured an inferior afterlife;
6. Through the death of Persephone, the death of human beings is somehow conquered.

These correspondences go a long way to explain why the Christian authorities were so hostile to mystery religions, which they saw as a real threat and rival.

Chapter 18
Alternative Systems

What we have examined so far under the heading of Greek religion has constituted devotion to a particular divinity or divinities at a single cult centre or sanctuary. As we have seen, 'mainstream' Greek religion consisted of a vast number of different cults and cult practices which the individual could move between, so to speak, depending more or less on individual temperament, social status, place of residence, family tradition, and so forth.

In this chapter, however, we are going to examine religious movements, which *did* constitute an exclusive form of worship and which were founded on an entirely different principle from that of ordinary Greek polytheism. They therefore represented, and were perceived to represent, a threat to conventional Greek religion in that they sought to undermine the communal life of the Greek *polis*, which operated on the notion that the *polis* is a religious community placed under the protection of a particular group of deities. The French scholar Marcel Detienne has detected a rejection of the central ritual of Greek religion, the sacrificial banquet, and hence a rejection of the *polis* itself, in the dietary taboos of both Pythagoreanism and Orphism. In addition, Pythagoreanism and Orphism embodied a set of beliefs or principles, which their adherents were *required* to uphold. Interestingly, both systems had their roots in the East. I should point out at the beginning that it is impossible to establish an entirely clear-cut distinction between the tenets of Pythagoreanism and Orphism: we just don't know enough about either.

Pythagoreanism

Pythagoras, the founder of Pythagoreanism, was born on the island of Samos in c. 570 BC. Much is attributed to him, including the invention of the musical scale and the famous theorem about right-angled triangles. His most important contribution to religion, however, was *metempsychôsis* (see p. 82). Pythagoras believed that he himself had undergone a number of incarnations and, as we have seen, was mocked by Xenophanes for believing that a human soul could reside in a dog.

For most of his life Pythagoras lived in the Greek cities of southern Italy, notably Croton, where he established a religious community. Under the government of this community Croton rose to political importance. A conspiracy, however, forced him to retire to Metapontum, where he died. At some date between 460 and 400 BC the community which he established was persecuted and almost wholly destroyed. The survivors succeeded in establishing themselves in Tarentum, which then became the seat of the movement until it faded away in the late fourth century BC.

The followers of Pythagoras were called *Pythagoreioi*. Membership was open to women and men. In order to qualify, you had to renounce all your private possessions and submit to a strictly regulated life. A five-year rule of silence was imposed on new members. If you later chose to renounce the order, you were regarded as a dead person and a gravestone was erected to commemorate your death. Pythagoreanism was based on a discipline of purity which was determined by the expectation of 'lives' to come. The level of existence that one attained in one's next incarnation was believed to be dependent upon the quality of one's life in one's present incarnation. The discipline was based on a set of prescriptions known as *akousmata* or 'things heard', which emanated from the teachings of Pythagoras himself. The *akousmata* included a prohibition on the eating of beans and certain parts of sacrificial animals, a preference for white garments, a ban on extramarital affairs, a prohibition on burial in woollen garments, a requirement to enter sanctuaries barefoot, a requirement to make one's bed after rising so that no trace of one's presence should remain, a prohibition on breaking bread and on picking up food which has fallen from the table 'because it belongs to the heroes', and so on. Some of the *akousmata* are reasonable and sound. Others, not to put too fine a point on it, seem a bit daft, as do most religious prescriptions to outsiders.

Greek religion normally placed very little emphasis on what a person should or should not do. Certainly it held no position on the large moral issues that dominate Christian debate today, such as divorce, abortion and contraception. As we have seen, sexual abstinence and purification were insisted upon for the duration of certain festivals, but only on a temporary basis. In Pythagoreanism, however, to quote Walter Burkert (*Greek Religion* 303), 'the alternating rhythm of the extraordinary and the normal is discarded and in its place there appears the opposition between the common, despicable world and the special, self-chosen life.' In this respect Pythagoreanism resembles monasticism.

Orphism

Orphism was supposedly founded by the divine musician Orpheus, who is said to have had the power to charm nature with his music-making. He is closely associated with Eurydice, for whom he descended to Hades after she was killed by a snake-bite. Hades agreed to release her on condition that Orpheus did not look back at her. Unfortunately he failed in this requirement and she was lost to him for ever. Another myth told how Orpheus was dismembered by Thracian women or maenads. His severed head floated singing on the water down to the island of Lesbos. This myth explains why Lesbos had such excellent lyric poets, including Sappho and Alcaeus.

Also central to Orphism was a myth about the origin of man. Zeus raped Rhea-Demeter and engendered Persephone. He then raped his daughter Persephone in the form of a snake and engendered Dionysos. Zeus gave the lordship of the world to Dionysos and had him guarded by the Korybantes. But jealous Hera sent the Titans to him and they distracted the infant with toys. While Dionysos was looking into a mirror, they killed the god, dismembered him, boiled him, roasted him and then devoured him. In revenge Zeus threw his thunderbolt at the Titans and incinerated them. From the rising soot man was born, while from the remains of his own dismembered body Dionysos was re-born. The myth apparently seeks to explain the origins of man's wicked nature, which it derives from the fact that he is descended from the Titans. Life for the first time in Greek religion becomes a penance for man's sinful origins.

Orphism constitutes the most problematic area of study within the whole field of Greek religion because it is practically impossible to distinguish what is genuine from what was foisted onto the movement in later times. In the fifth and fourth centuries BC there existed several religious poems ascribed to Orpheus called *Orphika*. This in itself represents an important departure in Greek religion, since books otherwise had little to do with practice and belief. The most important Orphic work was the *Rhapsodic Theogony*, which treated the origin of the gods differently from Hesiod's *Theogony* by giving a central position to a world-egg, out of which Phanes was born, creator and first king of the gods.

We know little about the contents of the *Orphika* but we can be fairly sure that they taught that the body (*sôma*) is the tomb (*sêma*) of the soul. Secondly, it is clear that vegetarianism was an essential rule of life. Orphics were not permitted to eat meat, beans, eggs, or to drink wine. Their dietary taboos were therefore far more extensive than those associated with Pythagoreanism. It seems that the Orphics also maintained that sins could be washed away by ritual means and initiation, and that a dualistic afterlife awaits us in Hades, although the evidence for this, since it comes from writers who are either contemptuous or critical of Orphism, can hardly be taken at face value. In what is probably a reference to Orphic belief, Aristophanes in the *Frogs* consigns to Everflowing Mud 'anyone who has ever wronged a guest...stolen money from a child, or thrashed his mother, or struck his father on the jaw, or sworn a false oath...' (145-50). For those who have led a virtuous life, on the other hand, the Orphic reward, according to Plato in the *Republic* (2.363c), is Everlasting Drunkenness. A little later in the same work he criticises those who

> ...produce a pile of books of Mousaios and Orpheus...in accordance with which they perform rituals, persuading not only individuals but states as well that there really is remission and purification for unjust behaviour by means of sacrifices and sportive delights for the living, whereas for the dead there are what they call rites, which deliver us from the evils of this world, while terrible things await us if we have failed to sacrifice.
>
> (2.364e-365a)

One has to conclude by admitting that the attempt to recover an ethical basis – if such ever existed – to Orphism is as ill-served by the prejudice of Plato as it is by the burlesque of Aristophanes.

Chapter 19
The Great Healer

I bring us now to one of the great healing centres in the world, to Epidaurus in the north-east Peloponnese, sacred to Asklepios. Epidaurus was originally the home of a certain Maleatas, a healing god who later became amalgamated with Apollo. Exactly when and how Asklepios arrived in Epidaurus is not known. Homer refers to him as a Thessalian king who knew the lore of healing, which he is said to have learnt from the Centaur Chiron. In myth Asklepios dies, indicative perhaps of the fact that medicine cannot transgress the laws of nature. He is said to have been killed by a thunderbolt shot by Zeus for having attempted to raise someone from the dead. Asklepios thus occupies an extremely unusual position in Greek religion, being a mortal who was subsequently promoted to the status of god.

The spread of the cult of Asklepios

Sickness and its cure were always a vital part of Greek religion, but it was only with the rise of the cult of Asklepios that the healing art was transferred to a major deity whose sphere of influence was devoted wholly to the healing art. We do not know exactly when that occurred, but the oldest votive inscription at Epidaurus should probably be dated to c. 500 BC. The cult initally only attracted local interest, probably due in part to the fact that it was exposed to political rivalries between Athens and Sparta.

The impetus behind its expansion seems to have been provided by the plague which inflicted Athens and no doubt other parts of Greece as well in the early 420s. In the fourth century BC a great deal of building was done at Epidaurus – at a time, it should be noted, when the level of building activity at other sanctuaries in the Greek world sharply declines. In other words, Asklepios' cult becomes important when the Olympian cults are not attracting financial investment on anything like the same scale which they had done from the seventh to the fifth centuries BC, the great age of Greek temple-building.

Epidaurus was just one of literally hundreds – probably some two hundred in all – of sanctuaries dedicated to Asklepios throughout the Greek world. Other important centres were at Athens, Kos, Pergamon and Rome, to name but a few. All were under the patronage of and to some extent the control of the sanctuary at Epidaurus. This in itself is an entirely new phenomenon in Greek religion, viz. a network of cults centrally administered. An inscription dated c. 365 BC lists numerous *theôrodokoi* or 'receivers of sacred ambassadors' who supported *theôroi* (sacred ambassadors) sent out by Epidaurus to promote new cults or collect funds. One is inevitably reminded of the apostles of the Early Christian Church.

The sanctuary at Epidaurus continued to be a healing centre until the Roman Empire officially recognised Christianity. The Emperor Julian the Apostate gave powerful support to Asklepios. Yet today Epidaurus lies totally in ruins. All that has survived is the theatre, due to the fact that it was covered by a landslip. The suspicion is that, like Eleusis, it may have been deliberately vandalised by the Christians, in this case because of the dangerous similarity between the person of Asklepios and that of Christ.

Incubation

Upon arrival at the sanctuary, the patient was required to perform a preliminary sacrifice before undergoing purification by ritual bathing. He or she then spent the night sleeping in the *abaton*, which means 'an unapproachable building', so-called because it was unapproachable to those who had not purified themselves before entering. It was hoped that while the patient slept the god would appear in a dream which would then be interpreted by a sanctuary attendant. This ritual is called 'incubation' in reference to the fact that the patient slept in the sanctuary. Alternatively the patient might be approached by a sacred snake. One of the most puzzling buildings at Epidaurus is the *thymelê*, a circular edifice or *tholos* consisting of an outer and inner colonnade (see Fig. 19). Beneath its floor are six concentric rings. We do not know what rites were performed here but one theory is that it housed the sacred snakes which were used in temple cures; another is that it is the tomb of Asklepios.

Aristophanes in the *Wealth* provides a comic description of incubation, which sheds an invaluable light on many of its details. In the following passage the speaker, a slave called Carion, is describing to his master's wife what happened when he went to the sanctuary of Asklepios in Athens in hopes that the god would cure the god Wealth of his blindness:

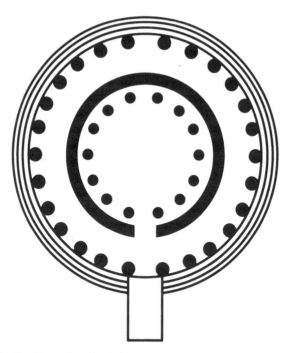

Fig. 19 Floor plan of a *tholos*.

When cakes and offerings had been consecrated on the altar and the fire had been nourished, we laid Wealth down in the customary manner and each of us made up our beds.... Then the god's attendant extinguished the lamps and told us to go to sleep and to keep quiet if anyone heard a noise. So we all lay down in the proper fashion.... I glanced up and saw the priest [of Asklepios] snatching the cakes and figs from the sacred table. After that he went around all the altars to see if any cakes were left and 'consecrated' them into a sack.... Then the god went around examining everyone's ailments in due order.... After this he sat down by Wealth and first he felt the latter's head, and then he took a clean linen cloth and wiped around his eyes. Panakeia [a daughter of Asklepios] covered the whole of his face with a scarlet cloth. Then the god whistled and two gigantic snakes wriggled out of the temple.... These slid underneath the linen cloth and licked Wealth's eyelids, so it seemed to me. And, dear lady, before you could have drunk ten goblets of wine, Wealth got up and saw. I clapped my hands for joy and

my master got up. The god made himself disappear and his
snakes vanished into the temple. You can imagine how those
lying by Wealth went on congratulating him and greeting him
until it became light.

(660-744)

Miracle cures

There are a number of inscriptions from Epidaurus dating to the second
half of the fourth century BC recording cures that are ascribed to
Asklepios. They tell us a great deal about the kind of ailments from which
the Greeks suffered. One of the commonest female complaints was
uterine disorder, as in the strange case of a girl called Kleo, which is
reported as follows:

> Kleo was pregnant for five years. After five years of pregnancy
> she came as a suppliant and slept in the *abaton*. As soon as she
> left and went outside the temple she gave birth to a son who
> immediately washed himself at the fountain and walked about
> with his mother. In gratitude for this she inscribed the following
> words on her offering: 'The size of this tablet is not a cause for
> wonder but the god is, seeing that Kleo carried her child in her
> womb for five years until she slept in the precinct and he
> restored her to health.'

> (*IG* IV² 1.121 no. 1)

No less miraculous is the following reported cure of blindness:

> A man came to the god as a suppliant who was so blind in one
> eye that all he had was an eyebrow with an empty eyesocket.
> Some of the people in the temple laughed at him for his
> stupidity at thinking that he would be able to see when the
> eyesocket was empty and contained nothing but a depression.
> When he slept, a vision appeared to him. The god was seen to
> be preparing some medicine and, opening the man's eyes,
> poured it over them. When day came he could see with both
> eyes and departed.

> (*IG* IV² 1.121 no. 9)

Anyone could come to Epidaurus seeking a cure for an ailment,
just as anyone can go to Lourdes in France today. And they evidently

came in their thousands. What percentage was cured is impossible to guess, but even one miraculous cure now and then would have been sufficient to keep hope alive – which was what Epidaurus, like Lourdes, was all about. I do not mean to sound cynical. After all, one's mental attitude towards illness may make the decisive difference in determining whether one is cured. But Epidaurus, in my view, was important not primarily because from time to time people were cured, but because it enabled the sick to go on hoping. Epidaurus, in other words, gave people the gift of being able to hope against hope, the gift of life.

Chapter 20
The Enlightenment and the Sophists

The beginning of the Classical period, conventionally dated 480 BC, coincides with a number of important intellectual developments which had such a profound influence upon Greek culture that scholars talk in terms of an 'Enlightenment'. The Enlightenment originated in the Greek cities on the western coast of Turkey and the offshore islands, and its roots were laid in the sixth century. Its importance is that it cast into question a number of fundamental assumptions about Greek religion. It was virulently iconoclastic. The leaders of the movement included some of the brightest and most radical thinkers that Greece ever produced. They did not constitute a unified group or school as such, although they did share a number of ideas in common. One was a determination to take a very hard look at what was done in the name of religion.

Xenophanes

The person who seems to have initiated the Enlightenment was Xeno-phanes, who lived in the second half of the sixth century BC and came from Kolophon. His statements included the following:

> Both Homer and Hesiod have attributed to the gods everything which brings shame and reproach among men: theft, adultery and mutual fraud.

> If oxen or horses or lions had hands or could paint a picture and create works of art like men, horses would draw pictures of gods like horses, oxen pictures of gods like oxen, and each species would make the body of its gods in accordance with its own appearance.

> The Ethiopians say their gods are snub-nosed and black-skinned, the Thracians that they are blue-eyed and red-headed.
> (*DK* 21 frr. 11, 15 and 16)

In other words, images of gods reflect the kind of people who create them. Man has created God in man's own image. Xenophanes was not, however, an atheist nor even an agnostic, for he declared his belief in:

> One god, one who is greatest among gods and among men who has neither a body nor a mind that resembles that of mortals.

(fr. 23)

He also maintained that there could be no certainty about what we profess to know about the nature of the gods:

> No man has ever known certainty nor will any man ever have certainty about the gods and all the things I mention. For even if he should chance to hit upon the exact truth he cannot know that he has done so. Appearance possesses everything.

(fr. 34)

Herakleitos

Another leading figure of the Enlightenment was Xenophanes' contemporary, Herakleitos of Ephesos (fl. 500 BC), one of whose more provocative statements was:

> The dead are nastier than dung.

(DK 22 fr. 96)

The implication behind this remark is that funerary procedure served no useful purpose at all. The dead are merely rotting matter, and particularly nasty rotting matter at that. Another fragment reads:

> Your character is your *daimôn* [guiding-spirit].

(fr. 119)

Herakleitos also challenged the worship of cult statues when he stated:

> Men pray to statues of the *daimones* although they cannot hear....

(fr. 128)

Like Xenophanes, Herakleitos was no atheist. Rather he believed in a god whose moral perspective was untainted by relativism. He wrote:

To god all things are beautiful, good and just; but men have
assumed some things to be just, others unjust.

(fr. 102)

The sophists

Xenophanes and Herakleitos and their contemporaries were not teachers.
They did not have pupils and they did not give instruction. But the
sophists, most of whom gravitated to Athens in the second half of the
fifth century, did. They made their livelihood by travelling from city to
city offering courses and giving lectures, primarily in rhetoric. They
taught the technique of how to win an argument, whatever the strength
or weakness of one's position. They professed to be able to train a young
man to argue with equal persuasiveness on both sides of a proposition.

The sophists make their appearance in response to the immense
importance that attached to public speaking in the Athenian assembly
and lawcourts. They are important for the history of Greek religion not
only, perhaps not primarily, because of their ideas, but because they
provided wealthy young men with the technical equipment to challenge
accepted practice and belief. One of the most celebrated sophists was
Protagoras (c. 485-415 BC), who was born at Abdera in Thrace. He
wrote:

Concerning the gods I am unable to discover whether they exist
or not; there are many obstacles to knowledge, the obscurity of
the subject and the brevity of human life.

(*DK* 80 fr. B4)

Another fragment states:

Man is the measure of all things. Of the being of things that are
and the non-being of things that are not.

(fr. B1)

Pericles, the most powerful politician in Athens from the mid-440s until
his death in 429 BC, collected around himself a circle of intellectuals
who shared such ideas. The leading member of this group was the
philosopher Anaxagoras, who declared:

All living things, both great and small, are controlled by Mind
(*Nous*)...and the kinds of things that were to be and that once

were but now are not, and all that now is and the kinds of things
that will be – all these are determined by Mind.

(DK 59 fr. 12)

Euripides and Aristophanes

These ideas came to a kind of fruition in the plays of Euripides. It is
possible, though we cannot be certain, that Euripides was an atheist since
he consistently presents the gods in an extremely negative light and
seems to call into question their entitlement to worship. In the *Hippolytus*, for instance, Aphrodite takes vengeance upon Hippolytus for his
neglect of her by destroying a perfectly innocent bystander, Phaedra,
who just happens to get caught in the crossfire. A member of the Chorus
says at the beginning: 'Gods should be wiser than human beings' (120).
But the precise point of the play is that they are not. In the *Bacchae*
Dionysos causes his aunt Agave to dismember her son Pentheus for
rejecting his divinity and claims to worship. It seems that Euripides is
either saying 'if the so-called gods behave like this, they are not gods'
or 'if the so-called gods behave like this, then god help us.'

Euripides not only questioned anthropomorphism as a basis for
religious belief but also alluded to the possibility that a single divine
being presided benignly over human affairs, as in the following prayer
which Hecuba, queen of Troy, utters in the *Trojan Women*:

> You who support the earth and occupy its seat, whoever you
> are, incapable of being comprehended, Zeus, or nature's necessity, or mind of man, I invoke you. Striding along a soundless
> path, you arrange all human affairs in accordance with right.

(884-9)

To which the simple-minded Chorus reply in complete bafflement:

> What do you mean? What a novel way to invoke the gods!

The cosmological theories of fifth-century philosophers are ridiculed in an extremely amusing scene in Aristophanes' *Clouds* where
Socrates 'proves' to the highly conventional Strepsiades that Zeus does
not exist and puts forward instead the theory that the world is governed
by an ordering principle called Necessity or Vortex (364-436).

Socrates

Socrates was born in Athens in c. 470 BC and died in 399. Plato repeatedly insists in his dialogues that Socrates was not a sophist, though the popular perception of him was that he did indeed belong to that movement. As just noted, Aristophanes makes him the focus of an attack upon the sophistic movement in the *Clouds*. Socrates was an educator like the sophists, though he did not charge for his services.

His religious beliefs are difficult to identify because he wrote nothing and we know him only from what Plato and others wrote about him.

He seems to have believed in a single divine power, even though in Plato's dialogues he also refers to 'the gods'. He too seems to have suspended any view about the afterlife, though it is quite clear that he did not believe in the conventional picture of Hades. At the end of the *Apology*, when he has been condemned to death, he says, 'So we part, you to life and I to death, but which of us goes to a happier fate, only god can know.' He attributed negative advice (negative in the sense that it told him what *not* to do) to his personal *daimonion* or little *daimôn*, which, for instance, told him not to go into politics. In the *Apology* he speaks highly respectfully of the Delphic oracle, and it is extremely unlikely that he mocked traditional observances in the way that some of the sophists did.

The evidence for a religious crisis

The Enlightenment, which had its roots in mid-sixth century Ionia, was disseminated in the next century by the sophists. It represented a challenge to traditional religion in the following ways:

1. It revealed a dissatisfaction with the view of the gods as anthropomorphic beings who resembled mankind physically and morally;
2. it indicated a desire to replace polytheism by an incipient monotheism;
3. it suggested an anthropological awareness that man creates god in his own image, i.e. that the Greek gods have the indelible stamp of Greekness upon them, whereas true divinity, if it exists, cannot be defined by Greekness or anything else;
4. it claimed that much of what people do in the name of

religion is silly; and finally,
5. it acknowledged that there is no certain knowledge of the divine.

I would emphasise that in all this there is little evidence of a movement towards atheism. Atheism was, however, undeniably in the air, being only a short step from the agnosticism that the sophists taught. One known atheist was Diagoras of Melos, who is said to have thrown a wooden statue of Herakles onto a fire which was dying out and proclaimed that the hero had performed a thirteenth labour by cooking the lentil soup that was simmering over it in a pot!

There were serious repercussions to what we have been discussing. Many people, it seems, got fed up with the Enlightenment. They had enough of clever-clever people telling them that their beliefs were stupid and that the moon was not in fact a god but just a lump of earth, which is actually what Anaxagoras stated. According to a law introduced by a seer called Diopeithes in c. 432 BC, the failure to acknowledge the state gods and the teaching of astronomy now became indictable offences (Plutarch, *Life of Pericles* 32). Those who are said to have been brought to trial on these charges include Protagoras, Diagoras, Euripides (unsuccessfully in his case), Anaxagoras and Socrates.

Conclusions

The challenge of the sophists notwithstanding, Greek polytheism continued to play a vital role in the ancient world, especially in Athens, until the sixth century AD. St Paul had no success at all when he visited Athens in c. AD 65 in hopes of converting its citizens to Christianity. In AD 395 Athens was reputedly saved from Alaric and the Visigoths by an epiphany of Athena and Achilles, who appeared, fully armed, on her city walls. It was only when the Emperor Justinian finally forbade any pagan to teach philosophy in AD 529 that Christianity, with the backing of an imperial fiat, truly won out over polytheism.

And yet there are signs of a change in attitude and practice from around the Peloponnesian War period onwards, and not just in relation to Athens. We see this, firstly, in a general encroachment by the civil authorities upon matters of a religious nature. That encroachment, though implemented for bureaucratic convenience, is visible especially in the growing involvement of the state in the financing of cults.

Secondly, the period from around c. 400 BC onwards witnesses a dramatic rise in heterodox and sectarian forms of religious worship whose association with Olympianism was marginal at most. The prime example of this tendency is the rise in popularity of Asklepios, who came closest to challenging the polytheistic basis of Greek religion and who, as we have seen, was destined to pose a serious challenge to Christianity.

Thirdly, there was a no less dramatic increase in the popularity of privately organised bands of worshippers known as *synousiastai, orgeônes, thiasôtai*, and the like, who constituted closed religious communities united in worship of a personal deity. Though these groups initially flourished more among metics (i.e. resident aliens) than among the citizen body, we need hardly doubt that they ultimately came to undermine the vitality of more traditional forms of civic worship. Examples of non-Greek deities whose cults proliferated throughout the Greek world include Bendis, a Thracian goddess whom the Greeks identified with Artemis, Adonis, the Egyptian goddess Isis, the Asiatic moon-god Mên, the Thraco-Phrygian god Sabazios, and many more besides. Though their initial entry seems to have aroused intense hostility as we know from uncomplimentary references to them in Aristophanic comedies, they gained ground none the less.

Fourthly, there was a no less dramatic rise in the popularity of mystery religions, notably the Eleusinian Mysteries. These reveal an extra-wordly orientation which essentially ran counter to Olympianism with its obsessive preoccupation with the here and now.

Finally, we may detect an increasing tendency upon the part of the educated élite to question the traditional gods and the basic tenets of polytheism. Though we cannot know to what extent their ideas filtered down to the citizen body as a whole, it is clear that at the end of the fifth century something akin to henotheism (i.e. a stage of belief between polytheism and monotheism when a single deity achieves prominent but not exclusive worship) was in the air, as manifested, for instance, by Hecuba's prayer to Zeus in the *Trojan Women* (p. 100), Sokrates' belief in his guiding spirit or *daimonion*, and the general dissatisfaction in intellectual circles with a system of belief that countenanced flagrantly immoral behaviour on the part of its gods. Diopeithes' decree notwithstanding, it is unlikely that these ideas simply went away.

Suggestions for Further Study

1. What does Homer's presentation of the gods in the *Iliad* tell us about the nature of Greek religion? How does he characterise the gods? What is the function of the scenes up on Mount Olympus? What impact do they have upon the action of the poem as a whole? What response do you think they evoked from Homer's audience?

2. What kind of relations were possible between mortals and gods? Think of all the ways in which these relations differed from those of the Christian or Jewish God towards their adherents. What is the basis of Athena's relationship with Odysseus and other members of his family in the *Odyssey*? On what occasions and with what purpose does she intervene in their affairs? How consistent is her intervention? Are there occasions when you might have expected her to intervene when she does not do so? If so, can you think of any explanation for this?

3. Does belief in divine intervention preclude belief in free-will? Or is it possible to believe in both simultaneously?

4. Why do you suppose the Greeks placed such a strong emphasis upon festivals, processions, games and their like? Was their religion merely a matter of outward show? In what ways might it have been personal and spiritual?

5. What is the basis of Euripides' complaints against the gods? Is it possible to learn anything much about Greek religion from his plays? Why do you suppose that so many of them end with a god appearing on stage to tie up all the loose ends? Discuss the character and behaviour of Dionysos in the *Bacchae*. Is the play an attack on religion or, conversely, a defence of it?

6. What strategies did Greek religion possess to intimidate and coerce its worshippers into a particular type of behaviour? Under what circumstances would it have availed itself of these strategies?

7. What evidence is there for dissatisfaction with the basic assumptions of Olympianism? Where dissatisfaction exists, who are its principal promoters? How successful were they in undermining its hold over the minds of the majority? To what extent were they able to set up rival forms of religious worship?

8. Why do you think that Greece produced no religious leaders of any note? What impact do you suppose that the absence of such leaders had on the development and character of Greek religion? What kind of a culture does produce religious leaders?

9. Why do you suppose that the Greeks had such an elaborate ritual for dealing with death and burial, when their beliefs about the afterlife were so indistinct and colourless?

10. What do the basic features of a Greek sanctuary have to tell us about the priorities of Greek religion?

Suggestions for Further Reading

Abbreviations

DK = H. Diels and W. Krantz, *Die Fragmente der Vorsokratiker*, 6th edn in 2 vols (Berlin 1951) [fragments of the Presocratic philosophers in Greek with translations and commentary in German; K. Freeman, *Ancilla to the Presocratic Philosophers* (Harvard reprint, 1983) provides an abridged version in English].
IG = *Inscriptiones Graecae* [the standard collection of Greek inscriptions].
LGS = *Leges Graecorum Sacrae* [selection of Greek inscriptions concerning religion].
OCT = Oxford Classical Text [standard edition of a Classical work].
SEG = *Supplementum Epigraphicum Graecum* [an ever-growing supplement to *IG*].
SIG = *Sylloge Inscriptionum Graecarum* [selection of Greek inscriptions].

General studies and handbooks

Bruit, L.B. and Schmitt, P.S., *Religion in the Ancient Greek City* (Cambridge, 1992) [intellectually challenging and abreast of the latest theoretical interpretations].

Burkert, W., *Greek Religion: Archaic and Classical* (Blackwell, 1985) [the standard reference work].

Dodds, E.R., *The Greeks and the Irrational* (Berkeley, 1951) [eccentric and quirky, but a work of genius].

Easterling, P.E. and Muir, J.V., *Greek Religion and Society* (Cambridge, 1985) [excellent introductions on art, sanctuaries, festivals, sophists, etc.].

Ferguson, J., *Among the Gods: an Archaeological Exploration of Ancient Greek Religion* (Routledge, 1989) [somewhat superficial treatment but contains much useful information].

Festugière, A.J., *Personal Religion among the Greeks* (Berkeley, 1954) [dated but still valuable].

Garland, R.S.J., *Introducing New Gods* (Duckworth and Cornell, 1992) [how and why cults came to be admitted into the Athenian pantheon].

Grant, F.C., *Hellenistic Religions* (Bobbs-Merrill, 1953) [useful sourcebook for the later period].

Mikalson, J.D., *Athenian Popular Religion* (North Carolina, 1983) [the identity of Athenian religion as practised by the common man].

Rice, D.G. and Stambaugh, J.E., *Sources for the Study of Greek Religion* (Scholars Press, 1979) [useful sourcebook].

Civilization of the Ancient Mediterranean (3 vols), (eds) M. Grant and R. Kitzinger (Charles Scribner's Sons, 1988) [contains many informative essays on cults, priesthoods, divination, sacrifice, the afterlife, festivals, etc.].

The Oxford Classical Dictionary (3rd edn forthcoming c. 1995) [contains numerous succinct entries on all central aspects of Greek religion].

Books and articles on specific topics

Burkert, W., *Ancient Mystery Cults* (Harvard, 1987) [the best scholarly introduction to Greek mystery religions].

Carpenter, T.H., *Art and Myth in Ancient Greece* (Thames & Hudson, 1991) [copiously illustrated guide to the depiction of the gods and heroes in Greek art].

Connor, W.R., 'Tribes, festivals and processions; civic ceremonial and political manipulation in archaic Greece', in *Journal of Hellenic Studies* 107 (1987) 40-50 [investigates the relationship between political advantage and religion].

Detienne, M., *Dionysos at Large* (Harvard, 1989) [brief but inspired investigation of the cult of Dionysos].

Davies, J.K., 'Religion and the state', in *Cambridge Ancient History* vol. IV, 2nd edn (Cambridge, 1988) 368-88 [excellent discussion of the place of religion in the Archaic state].

Faraone, C.A., *Talismans and Trojan Horses: Guardian Statues in Ancient Greek Myth and Ritual* (Oxford, 1992) [investigates the relationship between religion and magic and so incorporates much material not generally discussed in books on Greek religion].

Garland, R.S.J., *The Greek Way of Death* (Duckworth and Cornell, 1985) [death as a rite of passage].

———— *The Greek Way of Life* (Duckworth and Cornell, 1990) [ritual activity in connection with the life-cycle from conception to old age].

van Gennep, A., *The Rites of Passage* (French edn.,1909; reissued in English tr., Chicago, 1960) [the classic work on rites of passage].

Godwin, J., *Mystery Religions in the Ancient World* (London, 1981) [very useful brief survey].

Henrichs, A., 'Human sacrifice in Greek religion', in *Le sacrifice dans l'antiquité* (= *Entretiens Hardt* 27 [1981] 208-24) [fascinating study of a somewhat overlooked topic].

Kurtz, D.C. and Boardman, J., *Greek Burial Customs* (Thames & Hudson, 1971) [a standard investigation of the archaeological and literary evidence for death and burial].

Malkin, I., *Religion and Colonization in Ancient Greece* (= *Studies in Greek and Roman Religion*, vol. 3 [1987]) [the role of religion in the establishment of colonies].

Mikalson, J.D., *Honor Thy Gods: Popular Religion in Greek Tragedy* (North Carolina, 1991) [what characters and choruses in tragedy say about the gods].

Morris, I., *Death-Ritual and Social Structure in Classical Antiquity* (Princeton, 1992) [death-ritual as symbolic action and as a demonstration of social structure; methodologically-oriented but informative].

Parke, H.W., *Greek Oracles* (Hutchinson, 1967) [succinct and very readable description of oracular procedure].

——— *The Festivals of the Athenians* (Thames & Hudson, 1977) [calendar of festivals, discussed sequentially].

Parker, R., *Miasma* (Clarendon, 1983) [scholarly treatment of pollution-belief; assumes knowledge of Greek but accessible to non-Greek reader].

Rohde, E., *Psyche: The Cult of Souls and Belief in Immortality among the Ancient Greeks* (English translation 1925; reprinted Ares, 1987) [still the best work on the subject of death].

Simon, E., *Festivals of Attica* (Wisconsin, 1983) [brief but stimulating investigation of festivals].

Tomlinson, R.A., *Greek Architecture* (Classical World Series, Bristol Classical Press, 1989) [Companion volume in this series which contains a useful chapter on sanctuaries].

Vermeule, E., *Aspects of Death in Early Greek Art and Poetry* (Berkeley, 1979) [engaging and jaunty study with many modern parallels].

Vernant, J.-P., *Mortals and Immortals: Collected Essays of J.-P. Vernant*, (ed.) F.I. Zeitlin (Princeton, 1991) [essays by one of the most influential thinkers on Greek religion].

Ward, A.G. (ed.), *The Quest for Theseus* (London, 1970) [very readable essays on Athens' foremost hero].

Other books in the Classical World Series

Greek Tragedy
An Introduction
Marion Baldock

In this introduction to Greek tragedy, which constitutes some of the most powerful drama of the Western world, the author traces its development and performance with detailed chapters on each of the three tragic poets – Aeschylus, Sophocles and Euripides. Specific plays and topics are considered, and one chapter compares the differing treatment of the 'Electra' theme by each dramatist.

With illustrations, quotations from the plays in English, an annotated bibliography and suggestions for further study, *Greek Tragedy* is an invaluable guide to a study of the tragic genre.

Aristophanes and his Theatre of the Absurd
Paul Cartledge

Aristophanes, the Athenian comic dramatist, remains popular despite historical changes in attitude and belief. Placing the plays in their total civic, religious and dramatic context, this account explores their significance for contemporary audiences, and their continuing appeal. Separate chapters address aspects of his work and world, and attempt to outline the playwright's own opinions at a time of intense political debate.

With original texts quoted in translation this comprehensive and lively study will provide students with an invaluable insight into the plays and their place in classical Athens.

Religion and the Romans
Ken Dowden

This book provides a short, action-packed modern introduction to religion in the Roman world. It deals with the public and private nature of religion at Rome itself, and looks at the native cults of the Empire, with special reference to Gaul, as well as considering how the exotic cults such as those of Isis and Mithras were viewed. Finally, a fresh look is taken at the conflict of Christianity with the inhabitants and authorities of the Empire – from Nero to Constantine and beyond.

This lively and accessible book will prove invaluable to students of the classical world providing a much-needed general survey of Roman religion.

Morals and Values in Ancient Greece
John Ferguson

From the society of the Homeric poems through to the rise of Christianity, this account charts the progression of morals and values in the Greek world.

The author begins by discussing how a 'guilt-culture' superseded the old 'shame-culture' without totally displacing it. He then examines how democracy, the philosophers and finally Alexander's conquest influenced the values of the ancient Greeks.

Original texts are quoted in translation, and this clear, chronological study will provide an exciting introduction for students while offering experts a fresh approach to the subject.

Slavery in Classical Greece

N.R.E. Fisher

This is an authoritative and clearly written account of the main issues involved in the study of Greek slavery from Homeric times to the fourth century BC. It provides valuable insights into the fundamental place of slavery in the economies and social life of classical Greece, and includes penetrating analyses of the widely-held ancient ideological justifications of slavery.

A wide range of topics is covered, including chapters on the development of slavery from Homer to the classical period, on the peculiar form of community slaves (the helots) found in Sparta, on the economic functions and the treatment of slaves in Athens, and on the evidence for slaves' resistance. Throughout, the book shows how political and economic systems, ideas of national identity, work and gender, and indeed the fundamental nature of Greek civilization itself, were all profoundly affected by the fact that many of the Greek city-states were slave societies.

Classical Epic: Homer and Virgil

Richard Jenkyns

In the ancient world Homer was recognised as the fountain-head of culture. His poems, the *Iliad* and the *Odyssey*, were universally admired as examples of great literature which could never be surpassed.

In this new study, Richard Jenkyns re-examines the two Homeric epics and the work that is perhaps their closest rival, the *Aeneid* of Virgil. A wide range of topics is covered, including chapters on heroism and tragedy in the *Iliad*, morality in the *Odyssey* and Virgil's skilful reworking of elements from the two earlier epics.

Greece and the Persians

John Sharwood Smith

This account traces each stage of the critical struggle between the Persian Empire and the early Greek states, from the first clashes to the miraculous return home of 10,000 Greek mercenaries stranded in the heart of Persia.

Carefully examining sources and placing events within their geographical and historical contexts, the author attempts to define cultural and political differences between the two peoples. His balanced questioning approach places fresh emphasis on the Persian perspective and will provide an accessible and informed introduction to the period.

Athens Under the Tyrants

J.A. Smith

This study focuses on the colourful period of the Peisistratid tyranny in Athens. During these exciting years the great festivals were established, monumental buildings were erected, the population grew rapidly and there was lively progress in all the arts.

This study considers the artistic, archaeological and literary evidence for the period. Athens is seen largely through the eyes of Herodotus, the 'Father of History', and we can observe the foundations being laid for the growth of democracy in the following century.

Greek Architecture
R.A. Tomlinson

Greek Architecture is a clearly structured discussion of all the major buildings constructed by the Greeks, from houses to temples, theatres to Council buildings.

This book describes particular architectural styles and features and sets the buildings in their context, with an evaluation of their purpose, siting and planning.

With over 40 illustrations enhancing the text, *Greek Architecture* provides an informed and comprehensive view of the design and function of buildings in ancient Greece.

The Julio-Claudian Emperors
Thomas Wiedemann

'The dark, unrelenting Tiberius, the furious Caligula, the feeble Claudius, the profligate and cruel Nero...are condemned to everlasting infamy' wrote Gibbon. This 'infamy' has inspired the work of historians and novelists from Roman times to the present.

This book summarises political events during the reigns of Tiberius, Caligula, Claudius and Nero, and the civil wars of the 'year of four emperors'. It considers too the extent to which social factors influenced the imperial household.

Assuming no knowledge of Latin and drawing on material including inscriptions and coins, literary history and the latest historical interpretations, the author presents a coherent account of the often apparently erratic actions of these emperors.

The Attic Orators
Michael Edwards

The speeches of the Attic Orators were mostly composed for delivery in the Athenian law-courts and assembly, and at other public meetings such as state funerals, in the late fifth and fourth centuries BC. They contain much information about, and valuable insights into, the life, thought, and institutions of classical evidence for the development of Athenian prose literature. Yet, despite their undoubted interest, no extended survey of these speeches has appeared for almost a century.

This accessible book includes chapters on each of the ten Attic orators – their lives, literary style and works – as well as a survey of the origins of oratory in Greece. It provides students with a concise, up-to-date account which will, it is hoped, stimulate further study of some of the greatest works of literature produced by the ancient world.

Augustan Rome
Andrew Wallace-Hadrill

This well-illustrated introduction to Rome in the age of Augustus provides a fascinating insight into the social and physical contexts of Augustan politics and poetry, taking a detailed look at the impact of the new regime of government on society.

The ideas and environment manipulated by Augustus are explored, along with reactions to that manipulation.

Unlike more standard works on Augustus, this book places greater emphasis on the art and architecture of the time, and on Roman attitudes and values.

For further details of these and other Bristol Classical Press books please contact:

Gerald Duckworth & Co. Ltd
The Old Piano Factory
48 Hoxton Square, London N1 6PB
Tel 071 729 5986
Fax 071 729 0015